A Bed with a View

The experiences, sounds, sights,
conversations, thoughts, views and
memories of a hospital patient

PETER W BENNETT

Collated and edited by Karl French

Troubador Publishing Ltd
Unit E2 Airfield Business Park
Harrison Road, Market Harborough
Leicestershire LE16 7UL
Tel: 0116 279 2299
Email: books@troubador.co.uk
Web: www.troubador.co.uk

ISBN 978 1 80514 385 7

British Library Cataloguing in Publication Data.
A catalogue record for this book is available from the British Library.

Printed and bound by CPI Group (UK) Ltd, Croydon, CR0 4YY
Typeset in 11pt Minion Pro by Troubador Publishing Ltd, Leicester, UK

To my wonderful grandchildren
George, Tabitha and Emilia

"Say yes to life in spite of everything"
Victor Frankl

Contents

Introduction

This book was written a year before the coronavirus pandemic, which has shown us all (or perhaps reminded us of) the talent, commitment and heroism of our doctors, nurses and support staff. We proclaim, "Save our NHS", but I think in our celebration and exaltation, we perhaps fail to distinguish between the people involved, who must be praised unconditionally, and the vast organization that is the NHS that employs them.

We must be realistic about all of this, and we must remember that there were problems long before the pandemic. At the time of the junior doctors' strike, a doctor friend of mine told me, "Things must be bad for us to strike. It goes completely against our beliefs."

Prior to the pandemic, the NHS had long been subject to criticism, in a number of books, among them: Andrew Kay's *This is Going to Hurt*; Rachel Clarke's *Your Life in My Hands: A Junior Doctor's Story*; Sophie Petite-Zeman's *Doctor, What's Wrong?: Making the NHS Human Again*;

and Henry Marsh's *Do No Harm: Stories of Life, Death and Brain Surgery.*

As Fareeda Zakaria wrote in his book Ten Lessons for a Post-Pandemic World, "In October 2019, just a few months before the novel coronavirus swept the world, Johns Hopkins University released its first Global Health Security index, a comprehensive analysis of countries that were best prepared to handle an epidemic or pandemic. The United States ranked first overall, and Great Britain second. Both have performed miserably in confronting the pandemic, with their deaths per capita among the highest in the world.

There are few layman's accounts of what it is like to be a patient. So, as the world went into lockdown, I thought that this may not be the best time to write this book, but then, talking to some of the doctors who are risking, and indeed sacrificing their lives for us, one question is becoming ever-more important – will things be better off after a pandemic? This question is particularly pertinent as the vast organization that is the NHS has revealed weaknesses that were in fact evident long before the pandemic, and I suspect this crisis will not resolve or heal these problems, but it may merely conceal them.

While I am convinced that we must – always – recognize the many individuals whose extraordinary skills and bravery have saved so many lives, we must not allow our love and our gratitude to distract us from a serious, forensic examination of the NHS's broader strengths and weaknesses, and to do so with honesty and transparency, not least to ensure that our heroes' efforts are not wasted.

Since the very beginning of the pandemic, we have been repeatedly warned of the dangers facing us in countless newspaper articles, such as Claire Foges' piece in *The Times* of May 2nd, 2022, "Don't let faith in the NHS blind us to its faults", and I would also draw the reader's attention to David Aaronovitch's Times piece of May 14th, 2020, "Talk of angels and heroes avoids reality" and Anne Elisabeth Montet's article in the Telegraph of May 2nd, 2020, "We French love our health service but it's not a national treasure".

All of these writers and many more besides are exploring what remains an urgent subject, and this book is, at least in part, my contribution to the discussion.

1

Why Did I Write My First Book Aged 72?

Why did I write this book? I must say that, after eight drafts, many critical comments, and agents rejections, I have found myself asking the same question myself. The answer is, I think, some kind of compulsive literacy disorder. The chief symptom of this peculiar and debilitating condition is that you write a page or two and go to bed feeling rather pleased with your literary talent, only to wake the following morning, review the previous day's output and discover to your horror that it has by some miserable reverse alchemy been transformed into the work of a not-particularly-bright 10-year-old. I can never get to the bottom of the cause for this mental abstraction.

But, in truth, the real answer to that question is rather simple. It all started with my admission to hospital with some rather complex sinus surgery. I have to say that I was not a newcomer to the medical profession having spent the last fifteen years offering up my body to a roster of medical specialists to exhibit their unique skills. I had made it to the age of 72 having undergone 25 operations, engaging with surgeons specializing in neurology, ENT (12 sinus procedures), neck, knee, eyes and hip, and had done battle with bacteria that had proved unreasonably resistant to antibiotics, and a sleep disorder which caused me to sleep during the day, rather than night, which had a seriously negative effect on my social, family and sporting life. As a friend said, "You are supposed to give your body to science after you die. You have managed to do it during your lifetime."

Thankfully, all the surgeons had the good sense to render me unconscious to enable them to carry out their miraculous handiwork and to avoid my suggestions during the procedure. So, here I am, a former solicitor and businessman, married for almost 50 years, with two children and three grandchildren, enjoying life, in awe of the medical profession and fortunate to live in an age of extraordinary medical advances, blessed with a particular team of medical professionals of exceptional skill and dedication.

Most of my previous medical problems had been covered by private health insurance and my knowledge of the NHS was derived from listening to disingenuous politicians, hearing anecdotal evidence (positive and negative) from friends and watching the odd TV programme. I had also, as it happens, read a couple of medical books prior to this latest admission and have been a regular reader of "Medicine Balls" in *Private Eye* magazine. I had enjoyed both of the books for rather different reasons. Adam Kay's *This Is Going to Hurt* records the life of a junior doctor embarking on his medical career with a combination of humour, ignorance, lack of experience, anxiety, and sleep-deprivation, and the result is as funny as it is alarming and distressing. No wonder he left the profession to become a stand-up comedian. Henry Marsh's *Do No Harm* comes from the opposite end of the spectrum. In each chapter, one of the world's greatest neurosurgeons describes a surgical problem – and then the actual surgery – of immense complexity, requiring unique, ground-breaking surgical methods with the odds very often stacked against a successful outcome. Marsh is a genius, but an angry one, fulminating at the third-rate bureaucrats and politicians who get in the way of his life's work: saving lives. A depressingly inspiring book.

So, when I had cause to go into hospital, I thought it might be a good idea to write a journal from the patient's end of the bed. All the conversations and incidents in this book were written down in my diary immediately after taking place, allowing me to avoid distorted memories and to record my experiences accurately. However, the book turned out to be very different from my original concept of a simple, factual journal.

The hospital day – from 6am to 10pm – is stressful, noisy, sometimes painful, and the lack of sleep produces an almost hallucinogenic effect.

Long-forgotten memories of my earlier life returned like videos which appeared to calm, entertain and sustain me in this unfamiliar and distressing environment. So, a journal became a narrative and a stream of consciousness, a river of thoughts, ideas and reflections, both on my life and my time in the world.

Unfortunately, I have no recollection of my first experience of the medical profession, i.e. my birth. I was, to use the medical terminology, "delivered" on the 21st of November,1945, to Alf and Ada Dorothy (known as Ruby) Bennett. I have often wondered why the medical profession use the word "delivered", which to the rest of us, I believe, suggests the process of sending something through the post. In my dream-like state in hospital, I conjured up a scene of Alf and Ruby making their plans:

Alf: "Ruby, do you think we should order a baby."

Ruby: "I think it would be an excellent idea, although I am told that there is a long waiting list."

Alf: "Well, I've got the manufacturer's instructions here, so let me see what we have to do."

Ruby: "Do we have to pay a deposit?"

Alf: "I don't think so, but the leaflet includes diagrams of a series of most extraordinary physical activities to be undertaken...naked."

Ruby: "We're not biting off more than we can chew, are we?"

Alf: "I don't think so, my love, because the order only takes a few minutes to complete."

Their baby order – me – although delayed for nine months, was duly delivered.

To my amazement, when my brother researched our births, he found that the nunnery where I was born had actually kept the detailed records of my birth, which were as follows:

Ref No. 272, Admission 21.11.1945
History of previous pregnancies and confinements –
one forceps.
Born 21.11.1945 at 5.15pm, Dr Summers
Male alive ostermilk not
Discharged 5.12.1945
Remarks: Admitted in labour. Breech extended legs & arms, delivered eerily under GA placenta complete. Normal loss and stitches. Sutures in perineum.

Why a general anaesthetic? And why such a long stay in hospital?

I have always hoped that the 21st of November, 1945 might have been a day when a uniquely large number of great and famous people were born. Disappointingly, it was a quiet day for the potentially great and good and the only person of historical interest born on that day appears to have been Goldie Hawn, the American actress. This set me wondering if there might have been some kind of celestial error, and I had in fact been destined to be recognized as a literary superstar, and she merely to be known by fewer people than would fill a medium-sized pub on a busy Saturday evening.

My parents had bought a small semi-detached house in Litherland, Liverpool, where, interestingly, the poet Wilfred Owen had been stationed in the First World War. In 1939, the developers of the estate had the foresight to line the streets with trees which gave the modest house an arboreal canopy which greatly enhanced the environment. They were cut down many years later, presumably as a cost-cutting exercise.

I say the house was small but as a child one has a very different perspective and the house was my kingdom and my workshop in which an endless childhood was spent, along with a live-in best friend, my brother, building various military establishments and assorted pieces of hardware – tanks, aircraft-carriers, bombers, submarines – from the post-war furnishings available to us. I am delighted to report that when it came to major international conflicts, we remained the dominant world force.

My father worked in a timber-importing business. In fact, he *was* the business, the only employee of a long-established family company selling exotic woods, some of which were used in the building of Liverpool Cathedral. Because he was a salesman, we had a rarity: a car. He worked for the same company for one week short of fifty years, having started aged 15. My memories of him have never been positive. My recollection is of a chain-smoking depressive who spoke little, played almost no part in our lives, showed no emotional connection to my mother, was possibly an adulterer, silently did the *Daily Mail* crossword and whose only hobby was the Masonic Lodge.

He was a genuine chain-smoker, that is he lit the next

cigarette with the one he was smoking. In the evening, he would sit, speechless, next to a small desk which would contain a stock of cigarettes larger than our corner shop and guaranteed to keep the share price of his particular brand at an all-time high. He watched television and completed the crossword, and engaged in what was obviously a subconscious Freudian relationship with cigarettes. The transfer from an almost extinct nicotine assassin was a motion repeated robotically. As the extinguishing killer was about to set fire to his nose and lips, he would, without looking, pull out of the packet, positioned for easy access, and still without looking at it, the replacement lung-destroyer, which would be held briefly and tenderly as if to welcome it, and then be lit by the embers of its predecessor, placed in position, a deep breath inhaled, and then another plume of smoke would fill the small room.

My mother was also a heavy smoker, so when I had to have a chest X-ray a few years ago, the radiologist remarked that it was a miracle that neither my brother nor me had developed passive lung cancer. My brother and I have never smoked a cigarette.

As I have got older, I have tried to mitigate his apparent failings with the Christian virtue of forgiveness and a certain speculation as to why he was who he was. He had been in the navy during the Second World War and his brother, Will, had died when his ship was sunk, with the loss of 513 men. Did he perhaps suffer from depression, the treatment for which was then in its infancy? I just don't know, but in truth I remember him with little or no affection.

His smoking eventually killed him – he died of lung cancer before his 65th birthday. I really can't recall a time when he was well, as he had suffered from chronic emphysema for many years prior to his cancer diagnosis. He was admitted to a ward full of patients whose departure was inevitable, and therefore there was no reason to ban smoking. So it was that a group of cadaverous figures were sat together in death's smoky waiting room, lined up in cots, heavily drugged and, in my father's case, even more depressive and negative than before. He lingered in this grim, terminal state for many weeks and, as I was living in Northamptonshire at this time, I would drive up to comfort my mother and take her to visit him. However, as gloomy as it sounds – and as it was – each visit reminded me of a Liverpool characteristic that I will write about further: humour. On arriving at the hospital, we would get in the lift with other visitors coping with the tragedy of illness or death only to find that by the time we got out on floor 10 tragedy had somehow turned to comedy due to the comments of our fellow passengers. One I remember was a bloke saying in early spring: "I see the daffodils are out," to which the instant reply was, "Is it official or unofficial."

My father's parents (my grandparents) lived about a mile further away in a similar, small semi-detached house. My grandfather had spent his life working on the docks (more on this later) and was a small man, and as silent as my father. I have almost no memory of my grandmother beyond the fact that she was much bigger than my grandfather. It was said that on a Friday he would bring his wages home in a small brown envelope which she would open, give my grandfather his pocket money and keep the rest. They had four children: my father, his brother, Will (after whom I am named), and two daughters, Eunice and Olive. My grandmother died relatively young, my grandfather surviving her by many years.

Eunice, who had a large facial blemish – the result, it was rumoured, of a failed illegal abortion – had married Fred and they lived with my grandparents. Eunice herself died tragically young and Fred was never seen again after the funeral.

Olive was of a saintly disposition who had in fact considered the religious life, but instead married a watch salesman called Norman and lived in Dublin. She abstained from any form of alcohol to the extent that her "sherry trifle" was in fact just a "trifle". She also eschewed any form of modern equipment, e.g. a washing machine or a vacuum cleaner or indeed any form of heating, presumably on the basis that austerity was good for the soul. I only visited them once in Dublin with my wife and we both slept fully clothed (including an overcoat). She would periodically send my mother typewritten letters in which she would describe her pleasant, untroubled lifestyle. Whether she knew it or not, we certainly were aware that her husband, Norman, was a heavy drinker who would travel around Ireland selling his watches and getting volubly drunk before returning to a monastic existence in Dublin. Norman's modus vivendi reminds me of the story of that great Irish writer Brendan Behan who famously "liked a drop". In the morning he would walk to

9

his favourite pub in the centre of Dublin. On his way one of his neighbours would offer him "a quick one" which courtesy required him to accept until he reached the pub sufficiently drunk to write. One day he reached the pub sober, to the landlord's astonishment.

"Brendan," he enquired, "are you not at all well?"

"Bad news," Brendan replied, "the wife's signed me up for Alcoholics Anonymous."

"My God!" said the landlord, stunned into silence at the potential loss of trade. "How are you doing?"

"Not good," replied Brendan mournfully, "I'm having to drink under an assumed name."

Every Sunday, my father would take my grandfather to the pub and then bring him home for Sunday lunch. When I was old enough to drink, I was invited to join them, only to discover that conversation was not part of the outing. I assumed that this had been the case for the previous 30 years.

My grandfather lived well into his nineties. I remember him, when he must have been around 90, telling me that his doctor had recommended that he had eye surgery and he had given him an appointment in three years. It did appear to provide an incentive for him to survive, which he did with a simple sense of accomplishment and self-satisfaction.

The last time I saw my grandfather was a couple of weeks before Christmas 1976. He had survived my father by six months and decided to spend Christmas with Olive and Norman in Dublin. Two unusual events occurred. Firstly, he died. Apparently, he ate lunch and then expired. The perfect end, aged 96. Secondly, it emerged subsequently that he had changed his will shortly before he died. The previous will had left his modest estate to Olive and my father equally. In the new will, Olive was the sole beneficiary.

I knew that my mother would be devastated that, having provided him with Sunday lunch and generally kept an eye on him for more than 30 years, she had not been recognized. I rang Olive and suggested to her that she tell my mother that he had in fact left her a legacy of £1,000 to thank her for everything she had done for him. Olive refused as she believed this would be not telling the truth. I called her again and informed her that I would be furnishing the £1,000 so that she would not be out of pocket. Again, she refused. My mother was, as predicted, deeply upset. So much for Christian charity and compassion.

In accordance with established family practice, as soon as Olive died Norman disappeared and we heard years later that he was living in Andorra and that he had a child born before he married Olive. I don't know whether Olive herself knew anything of this serious breach of the rule of chastity.

Anyway, my grandfather's death did provide a particularly bizarre funeral. He was interred in an Irish coffin, which was duly transported to Liverpool for the funeral. The weather matched the solemnity of the occasion: it was freezing. We reached the part of the funeral where the coffin is lowered into the prepared grave. Alas, the gravediggers had forgotten that an Irish coffin is slightly wider than the English one, so it got stuck on its outer edges and hung helplessly at ground level. As we got colder, one of the gravediggers got the idea that if he stood on it, it might be released and so descend to its required position. Unfortunately, the coffin proved unstable, and we watched in horror as a small man with soiled hands rode the coffin like a surfer on a surfboard. As hypothermia was starting to set in, he decided to abandon ship but the action of him abruptly stepping off the coffin caused it to pivot at once into a vertical position, causing a muffled sound to emerge from within. My grandfather had never been an especially active man the shocked silence that enveloped the mourners was finally punctured by somebody declaring, "Christ, he's taken more exercise since he died than when he was alive."

By this time, the vicar in his light vestments was close to requiring an ambulance to take him to A&E, so we left grandfather's coffin standing like a memorial in a war cemetery. Bless him, he had served his country and lost a son fighting for it – he deserved a unique end.

I adored my mother and of course still do. Where my father was depressive and negative, she was the opposite, a positive, optimistic woman who exuded total, unconditional love for my brother and me, both emotionally and practically. When I would produce some wild fantasy about my future success, my father's retort was, "You'll come a cropper one day." Whereas my mother would pour fuel on the flames of any of my ambitions and abstractions, however fanciful. She encouraged me to believe, to dream big dreams, and she would reinforce her view by, for example, if we passed a big house, saying, "That's the sort of house you will live in." Later, she would give me money to buy a good-quality shirt or pair of shoes as I "would become somebody". Later in life, after I had attained some modest success, I bought an expensive car. I took her for a ride during which both electric windows failed to close, and it started to rain. After a few miles we were both drenched, her hair and clothes soaked. I know precisely what my father's comment would have been, but she was unable to say anything negative, so smiled and said with her soft Liverpudlian accent, "You've done really well, son."

I owe her so much but, tragically, she died too young, after a number of years of ill health following the death of my father. She had always been quite delicate, having suffered badly with rheumatic fever as a child. However, she had a big personality. She had that Irish ability to tell a good story, and my friends always liked visiting our house because of her warmth and geniality.

My first question is: why did my parents marry at all? They were so different and showed no signs – verbal or physical – of attachment to each other. My mother did once say that she had been in love with my father's brother, Will, but she married my father because he was "safer" and Will was wilder. Of course, if she had married Will, I would not exist. This decision was almost certainly regretted, as my father was apparently something of a womanizer, which accounted for my mother's overwhelming devotion to her sons and the extremely close relationship she retained with her mother who would visit us daily when my father was out and leave before he returned. Looking back, she always had an aura of sadness which I failed to appreciate, let alone understand.

Central to her life was a real "Agatha Christie" mystery. Her father was an Irishman named Daniel Leahy who was born around January 1886. I say *around* because at least three times during his life, including in his naval records, he seemed to have changed the date. Little is known of his background but my brother, John, and sister-in-law, Diane, are the family historians, and it appears that he and his sister Mary were born Catholics as evidenced by their Catholic birth certificates [insert copies]. However, on the 5th of September, 1898, Daniel and his sister were baptised into the Protestant Church [insert copy]. It's believed that this was to allow Mary to attend a Protestant school in Liverpool and improve Daniel's career prospects.

In any event, he went to work, aged about 14, in the home of a doctor in London and subsequently joined the Merchant Navy. He married my grandmother, Ada Rigby, in 1914. Unfortunately, he turned out to be a scoundrel. He sailed the seven seas, returning occasionally – on one of these occasions with enough money to buy a pleasant house overlooking the Mersey – and bringing mother exotic presents from around the world. Later, they had to sell the house, and so my mother and grandmother were forced to move in with my great-grandmother who lived in a tiny, terraced house without any electricity or gas and with an outside toilet, where they remained – in the house, that is, not the toilet – until my mother married and

14

my grandmother died. I remember with great affection staying in the house as a child. It had a magical feel to it. You entered into a narrow corridor off which, to the right, was a small room full of the presents that Daniel had brought home from his travels. I recall in particular a large ceramic doll and a beautiful silk screen which I was told had come from India. The room was like a junk- or antique shop. You then went into a meagre living room which was dominated by the fireplace flanked by the ovens in which my grandmother cooked whatever was available on the household income. At the back was the kitchen, in which she hand-washed clothes – there was a wooden mangle or wringer which I loved to hand-crank. There was a tight, little set of wooden stairs that led up to two small bedrooms. One of these was where my grandmother and I slept with a potty under the bed to avoid the journey to the toilet in the yard for our overnight emergencies. In the other room were two wooden chests which contained her late husband Daniel Leahy's effects which had been returned following his mysterious death on board the *SS Duchess of Bedford* on the 14th of October, 1939. My grandmother never touched the chests nor, indeed, mentioned them or Daniel whose name was, in fact, never uttered by any member of the family. My brother and I would occasionally, if alone, open the chests to discover a vast array of items described later. Our attention was drawn to our unspoken-of grandfather by the fact that he did not appear in our parents' wedding photographs. We were told that, quite simply, he was due back from India, but his ship had not arrived in time. No further questions admitted.

It was only when my brother and his wife were researching family history that the truth – or perhaps some kind of informed speculation – revealed Daniel's extraordinary end. On the date of my parents' wedding, the records disclose that he was in fact not travelling towards Liverpool but away from it and had died on the 14th of October from poisoning. When John and Diane searched the Merchant Navy's records, they found, to their astonishment, a long hand-written report of the last days of his life.

I find it amazing that this document exists, relating to a "bedroom steward". Was he poisoned or was his death accidental? But his behaviour from the time he attended the ship's surgery on the 12th of October and his sudden death on the 14th is certainly suspicious. The report records, his belongings were itemized and returned, and they remained in my grandmother's box room, never to be opened.

When my brother and I reached our teens in the early '60s, our mother had one overwhelming, all-consuming fear: that we should get a girl in trouble. It should be remembered that this was a time just before the pill and the era of free love.

She would daily, as we ate our tea, warn us of the dire consequences, while wielding a large bread knife. At that time, to conceive a child out of wedlock was the worst social disgrace that could befall a family of our social class, leading to acts of cruelty that we now look back upon with horror, whereby young, unmarried mothers and their children would be forcibly separated.

My mother was a simple soul, having left school at 14, and shared with many the blind, irrational, nonsensical and prejudicial views about others, particularly Catholics. Neither she nor my father showed any interest in the spiritual life, never attended church or alluded to any Christian teaching, save for strongly encouraging chastity for practical reasons. It must be remembered that in the 1960s in Liverpool, the Catholic-Protestant divide was an open sore in society. The orange and green marches were enthusiastically supported, and areas were inhabited by predominantly one domination or the other. We didn't have Catholic neighbours, and children were educated along religious lines.

My mother's other major fear was that John or I might become involved with a Catholic girl. I seriously believe that if we had brought a Catholic girl home it might have been too much for her already weakened heart. So, it was her bounden duty to warn us – again, daily – against such a liaison on the basis that Catholic girls did "unspeakable things", the emphasis being on the word *unspeakable*. When we enquired what these unspeakable activities might be, she would go pale and say that she could not tell us about them as they were "so unspeakable". This, inevitably, just served to arouse our curiosity but, because of the scarcity – absence of opportunity, we never entered that particular circle of Dante's Hell.

My mother's other absurdly farcical view was that she could tell a Catholic by the way they walked. When asked for the core, physical evidence, she would merely reply, "Just trust me. I know!" After some detailed research, I myself never managed to spot the key signs. I wonder what she is thinking now, knowing that I eventually became a Catholic convert. Maybe she would know by the way I walk."

As I reflect on her eccentric views on Catholicism, I recognise a force for good in her attempts at the teaching of sexual mores. Looking back, we lived in an age of innocence. No internet flooded with pornography confusing young people as to how sexual relationships should be conducted with respect, mutual understanding, kindness, and the lack of fear on the part of women as to men's motives and actions. My mother was our moral guide. No sex lessons at school, and my one nervous attempt to raise the topic with my father produced one of his famously abrupt responses: "Women are involved." *The Naturalist* and the double seats at the local cinema provided some anatomical details necessary, but how to treat the opposite sex was down to my mother's simple rules, repeated often and with a seriousness unlike her normal character. Although she lacked the freedom a modern woman would have, I look back on her as a feminist. Her model for my brother and me was simple: 1) you treat girls with respect, as equals and are there to protect them; 2) in practical terms, this simple formula was exhibited in a number of ways – a) when out walking, always walk on the outside of your female companion, b) always open a door to allow a woman to walk through first, c) always stand up when a woman enters the room, d) do not use bad language in front of a woman, e) respect her wishes in any physical activity and do not allow your passions ("I know men," she would say) to cause a girl to be in any way upset.

"Respect" was her mantra which I hope has stood me in good stead, and certainly allowed me, since my initial contact with my female sixth-form colleagues, to see women as friends rather than as sexual objects, notwithstanding a natural male admiration for their God-given beauty.

In the maelstrom of views that now circulate in society, I suspect my mother's views will appear to be antiquated and simplistic. But have things changed for the better? Opening the paper every day, I fear not. Peter Doggett's recent book *Growing Up: Sex in the Sixties* exposes the dangers of the liberation philosophy that emerged from that decade of "free love" in which my mother's mantra of respect appears to have been lost.

Sadly, once my father died and John and I had left home, her health deteriorated, and she kept collapsing at home. An ambulance would take her to hospital, they would check her over and send her home. Depression was the diagnosis. I would travel up from Northamptonshire to see her as often as I could, but the fainting continued. We were so blessed that her neighbours Edie and Joyce Cornes showed her love and practical help of biblical proportions.

Her medical problem did provide one interesting encounter with a medical consultant in Liverpool. To try and help her, I arranged to take her to be seen by a number of consultants, privately, in Rodney Street, Liverpool's Harley Street. For my mother, visiting a consultant was like meeting royalty. She had her hair done and wore her finest. After she arrived, she was ushered in to see the doctor. After a few minutes, the door of the consulting room opened and my mother appeared, looking rather shaken. She beckoned me over. I entered the consulting room to find the doctor lying peacefully on the desk, sound asleep.

"What happened, Mum?" I said, stunned by the scene.

"He asked me how long I had been pregnant, then put arm and head on the desk and went to sleep," she stammered. "Should we wake him?"

"Best left, I think," I said as calmly as possible, taking her arm and leading her out.

"The doctor seems to have gone to sleep," I said to the secretary who, strangely, did not seem to be as shocked as we were.

"He's been under a lot of stress recently," she replied, and we left.

We learned later that he was suspended for his drinking, and we were relieved not to receive an account. One Sunday, the 7th of September, 1980, I received a phone call which resulted in my only brush with of what I can call the super-natural. My mother had been admitted to hospital yet again. I had seen her the previous Wednesday, but I suddenly developed the strong feeling that I should go and see her again. But then I reasoned that she would, no doubt, be out the next day as usual. However, the instinct to go persisted and indeed became only stronger. So, I drove up to Liverpool and found her in a bed in the hospital, very sleepy. I was told that they had given her some medication to calm her down and that there was nothing to worry about. I sat on the bed, she opened her eyes, smiled the smile I had known since I was a child and said, "I love you, son."

"I love you, Mum," I said, kissing her, and left.

The following morning, the phone rang in my office to say she was dying, and I should get to the hospital. I drove to Liverpool as fast as I legally could, but I arrived too late. An autopsy revealed that she had not been depressed but had been suffering from a rare heart condition which had been undetected throughout her final years. She had never complained to me. She was not only the most loving mum a man could have, but also the bravest. God bless her.

As I write about her, I realise how little I knew of her or indeed of any of my forebears. There are popular TV shows that reveal to participating celebrities details of their family histories, which invariably come as a complete surprise to them. I knew my father and mother as parents, not as individual personalities. I never had a conversation with my father about his past, his interests (which appeared to be solely the Masonic Lodge), or any subject of general or topical interest. I did talk to my mother, yet it was never about her but about me, as she comforted me and encouraged me during my teenage years. After starting university aged 18, I never really ever lived at home again and got on with the business of enjoying life, exploring and finding a way of making a living. I suspect we only get to know our parents as individuals if they live long enough – and we ourselves mature – to engage in adult conversations or if we are part of a large family where family secrets are shared. Sadly, neither of these applied to me as both my parents died young, and I had no cousins. Strangely, I reflect now, although I love my brother and we have spoken at least once a week all our lives, we have never shared our views about our parents. Would they be the same?

> "Love as powerful as your mother's for you leaves its own mark. To have been loved so deeply, even though the person is gone will give us some protection forever."
>
> J. K. Rowling, *Harry Potter and the Philosopher's Stone*

2

Viva España

My medical problems, treatments and surgeries have been many and varied. However, I have had one consistent complaint throughout my medical odyssey. For more than 30 years I have suffered from chronic sinusitis. It was originally diagnosed by a brilliant ENT surgeon, Grant Bates in Oxford, who became a friend, but who died tragically young. He undertook my first sinus operation and warned that the problem would likely return two years later. He was right about that, and so two years later we had our second attempt, known in the trade as a "wash out". Sinusitis appears to be something of a mystery to the medical profession because of its ability to reappear on a regular basis and, in my case, be resistant to antibiotics. So, rather like competitors at a biannual sports event, the team was back in business. As I have said, Grant, an outstanding man as well as a brilliant surgeon, died and, before doing so, recommended a colleague to manage my disobedient sinuses. He proved to be a quite brilliant choice but, as the years passed, the infections became more frequent, requiring more surgery. Eventually, in May 2018, my surgical artist, who I dubbed "The Picasso of Sinuses", decided on the nuclear option, known by the unforgettable title of The Endoscopic Modified Lothrop Draf III Procedure which basically involves removing all of the channels from the frontal sinuses (which are above our eyes), leaving a large space for any infected material to escape unhindered by narrow channels.

The operation appeared to be a success, but in September the God of Sinuses decided that he had not finished with me after all, and I became re-infected. A full-scall antibiotic barrage was undertaken, gradually increasing in firepower and eventually resorting to two hospital admissions of a week each for the antibiotic to be administered intravenously.

Whilst this was happening, my wife, Sarah, and I had arranged a week's holiday with my son Tom, his wife, Annie, and three grandchildren, George, Tabby and Emilia in Sotogrande in Southern Spain. Stents had been inserted into my nasal passages to ease drainage, and I was told that there was one antibiotic left that could be administered outside of a hospital for a week, but if it failed to work, I would have to fly home to be admitted to hospital.

So, we settled into a hotel near where my son and family lived, in the hope that the antibiotics would work. Alas, they didn't, and I became ill, and consultations ensued between Picasso and a Spanish consultant who agreed that the first thing to do was to immediately take out the stents. It was at this point that I discovered that the British and Spanish approaches to surgery were markedly different. In the UK, any examination or treatment of the sinuses is preceded by a small amount of anaesthetic being squirted up the nose to alleviate any discomfort. Unfortunately, my non-existent Spanish failed to communicate the benefits of this practice to my non-English-speaking surgeon who suddenly produced what I took to be a pair of garden pliers, and, accompanied by the sound of an English coward crying, duly removed the stents. I still believe that the loss of the Armada and the Gibraltar dispute may have provided a subconscious motive. In pain, I left the hospital and returned to the hotel to rest. Suddenly, there was a heavy knock on the door and an obviously distraught young Spaniard handed me a note written in pidgin English which said, "Yu wif is ded in poole cum wif me." I raced to the swimming pool to find that Sarah was very much not "ded", but lying on a bed with her leg up, in severe pain. As we approached her, we were told to avoid the floor as it was slippery. It was, in fact, so slippery that it would have put Torvill and Dean's "Bolero" routine in jeopardy. It soon emerged that Sarah appeared to have slipped and broken her thigh. An ambulance arrived and she was taken to the local public hospital which had the appearance of a First World War field hospital with patients scattered around the place on various beds, surrounded by friends and family, eating and talking quickly and animatedly as the Spanish are wont to do. No member of staff spoke English, but I was confident that my well-earned reputation in "Charades" would provide the method of communicating the simple fact that Sarah was in a great deal of pain. After what I considered was an outstanding performance, with a clear and unambiguous message, I was shown to the men's toilet.

Fortunately, my daughter-in-law, Annie, who speaks fluent Spanish, arrived and, with my son, Tom, spoke to the nurse whose only use up to that point had been to show me to the toilet.

Under our travel insurance policy, Sarah was entitled to be transferred to a private hospital. Simple. Or so you would think. Put her in an ambulance and take her there. But, no! Presumably for some socio-political reason, the ambulance-drivers at the public hospital refused. OK, so let's not panic. Get a private ambulance service to take her. Simple. No! The private companies would not accept cash and you had to have a special card to show the driver which we didn't have. We were stymied, until Annie addressed the ambulance-drivers. To this day none of us knows exactly what she said to them, but it seemed that the feminist movement had not taken root in this remote part of Andalusia, and with a look that combined fear and contempt, one stepped forward reluctantly to drive us to the private hospital. Sarah was strapped in the ambulance, and I sat beside her. It immediately became apparent that revenge was in the air, particularly from this ambulance-driver who, I suspect, had a passion for bullfighting and who had endured a tongue-lashing from an ENGLISH WOMAN. He drove at Formula 1 speed, hitting every kerb and obstacle en route, thus causing as much discomfort as possible.

Sarah was unloaded from the ambulance into a private room in the private hospital and the diagnosis was that she needed a new hip. Alas, they didn't have a replacement in her size, but one would be obtained as soon as possible from Seville, 60 miles away. She lay there for three days, with her damaged leg extended and to which was attached a weight hanging over the end of the bed to keep the leg immobile. None of the staff spoke English but out of the mist of incomprehension came the Spanish Asclepius (the God of Medicine). He was young and looked like Julio Iglesias. He was, he told us, a surgeon with an outstanding reputation for hip replacements. He took hold of Sarah's hand and declared in perfect English, "I am here to heal you, to make you perfect again, to restore the beauty of your leg. We will do it together, and I shall not leave you until, with God's help, I am happy that YOU (with a long emphasis on *you*) are happy. So, then we are both happy and will thank the Lord."

I must say I found it difficult to hold back the tears. We NEVER saw him again.

I spent several days lying on a couch with a severe headache, taking antibiotics and feeling ever-more unwell. People would appear (presumably some of whom were doctors), talk to my wife in Spanish and disappear. Nobody ever appeared to attempt speaking English to her either because they couldn't or their history lesson about the Spanish Armada had left deep subconscious scars. The food was inedible.

Late on the third evening, Tom and I were sitting with her when a man arrived looking like a gypsy. He disconnected the bed and started to wheel it, and Sarah, out of the room. What was happening? For a moment, I suspected a kidnap attempt, but surely not from a hospital. It was 10pm and we discovered that she was being taken for surgery, which would take a couple of hours, after which she would be in the recovery room, and we should not expect to see her until probably 3am when she would be sleepy. So, it would be sensible to go back home and see her in the morning.

She was taken into the operating room and met by a team of young Spanish surgeons and an anaesthetist. Julio Iglesias obviously had a singing engagement. With limited English, she was told that she would not have a general anaesthetic as is common in this country, but an epidural. A screen was placed between her upper and lower body and in due course the surgical conquistador, equipped with tools normally found in a butcher's shop, set about the job. The anaesthetist indicated that he might not be able to be present throughout the procedure as he had a supper date. Sarah said that the noise of the hammers, drills and other items involved was deafening, and over the screen she could see the orthopaedic matador wielding his tackle with Herculean enthusiasm.

As she told us in the morning, the operation was completed at about midnight and she expected, as we had been told, to be in the recovery room for several hours. However, following the procedure, and due either to exhaustion or hunger (remember the Spanish eat late), the medical team decided to miss out the "recovery" phase and take her back to her room.

In this country, following hip surgery, which I have had, the patient is up the following day, exercising with physiotherapists, and as soon as you can go up and down stairs with crutches you are sent home. Not in Spain. There, you stay in hospital for, in Sarah's case, five days and on release are given a zimmer frame to use for at least two weeks. Fortunately, she could stay with my son and family for the month before she could be repatriated.

I flew home for my own admission to hospital.

"Take my advice and live for a long time.
Because the maddest thing a man can do in
this life is to let himself die."
Miguel de Cervantes, *Don Quixote*

3

I Begin My Medical Magical Mystery Tour

Day One – Thursday 1st November, 2018

To start this Medical Magical Mystery Tour, the NHS went out of its way to ensure I was going turn up and take part!

I had received three identical letters reminding me of my admission, each with pamphlets giving me information as to how to get to the hospital and where to park and lots more besides. There was also a recorded message on my home phone, which instructed me to "press 1" if I was Peter Bennett and then reminded me of the admission yet again.

I arrived at the hospital at 7.30am, having – as instructed, not eaten for 12 hours, and desperately worried about Sarah. The surgery started at 3pm and was unusual and complex, requiring two holes to be drilled in my forehead and the insertion of two bolts, which could be opened in order that cleaning fluids could be poured directly into my frontal sinuses. I suggested that Domestos might do the job as it was excellent at home in the sink and the toilet, and my surgeon, who is brilliant and has operated on me eight times already, appreciated my rather surreal sense of humour.

Before any surgery, you are asked to sign a consent form, which I have always done without ever reading it. However, this time my surgeon asked me whether I was happy for students to watch the operation.

"Of course," I replied. "I always perform better with an audience."

After the operation, the "Picasso of Sinuses" came to see me, and I asked him if we had drawn a good crowd.

"Full house," he said proudly, but modestly, "it is an unusual procedure."

"Splendid," I replied woozily. "Did you get a standing ovation? Did they demand an encore?"

When I was returned to a small, six-bed ward, it was already about 8pm and I was rather anxious to ring my wife, as I knew she would be worried. However, somewhere along the line my mobile had been lost. I asked one of the nurses if he could kindly ring her to tell her that everything had gone well, and I was OK. He agreed without hesitation.

After 30 minutes, there was no sign of the nurse, and I was starting to get agitated, so I asked another nurse who said she would make enquiries. She returned about 15 minutes later to tell me that the first nurse had not been able to make the call as he was dealing with a patient's discharge.

"Not life-and-death," I said angrily. "My wife will be desperately worried, and it would have only taken 30 seconds for the nurse to come and tell me that he had not got through."

The nurse then told me that the original nurse was in fact dealing with an urgent case (presumably having finished the discharge) and had had no lunch. "But couldn't he ask another nurse to come and tell me," I asked angrily, expressing my feelings strongly and emotionally.

10.30pm   I ask for a urine bottle. The nurse brings two, and I manage to fill both.

11.00pm   Food arrives, 27 hours after my last meal! It is a sandwich, two apples in a paper bag and a small plastic carton of orange juice

11.30pm   The ward sister arrives, and I apologise for being aggressive earlier. I tell of her of my wife's situation. She is sympathetic, but still no call is made.

11.40pm   A nurse arrives and asks about my pain level. I say 5 out of 10. She says she will get some codeine. I never see her again.

12.00pm   No sign of anybody. The food bag and the two bottles of now-vintage urine are on the table next to my bed, which I cannot reach. I am starving and finding that the two large bottles of urine (notwithstanding it is my own) are beginning to ferment and secrete a nauseous smell that is making me feel sick.

12.15am   I ask if there is any chance of some more food.

1.00am   They start the intravenous injections which involve antibiotics in a bag above my head, dripping slowly into a cannula in my arm. It takes about 40 minutes and would now have to be done three times a day.

I never got through to my wife until the morning.

The nurse tells me that the hospital is understaffed, and that they are recruiting 25 new nurses from India. She sees my collection of books which include Marsh's *Do No Harm*, which she tells me she has read, and that it had made her cry. I ask her if she reads a lot.

She says, "No, I'm always too tired."

1.30am   Food arrives, the same as before, a sandwich and two apples in a paper bag. I cannot sleep. It doesn't seem to have been the most promising start.

One of the new experiences of being in a ward with randomly selected fellow patients is to get an insight into other people's lives, which in normal circumstances I would never have done. The bed opposite was occupied by a Liverpudlian who had a pronounced Scouse accent. The phone went and his wife or partner opened the conversation. The phone was on speaker. Why must everyone speak on the speakerphone now? Anyway, the conversation went as follows:

Wife:	"When will you be home?"
Patient:	"By Wednesday, I hope."
Wife:	"Well, for Christ's sake, be home by Friday to pick up the benefits. And don't forget to tell them we've got another kid."
Patient:	"But, we haven't. Damien isn't due until January."
Wife:	"Haven't you ever heard of a premature birth, you stupid bastard?"
Patient:	"I thought it was premature ejaculation."
Wife:	"Well, with six kids you've been fuckin' useless at that. And don't forget to get the form for me stress anxiety."
Patient:	"What's that for?"
Wife:	"Being married to a lazy fucker like you!"

He left on the Thursday to continue what, I trust, was a long and happy relationship.

Friday 2nd November, 2018

My first full day on the ward is quite a revelation, as more staff appear, and the hospital comes to life.

6.00am	The staff today are an international crew. Spanish, Italian, Romanian and Filipino. All very pleasant and professional.
7.00am	Breakfast is Weetabix, small orange juice, coffee and toast – if you asked for it.

9.30am   My surgeon arrives with one of his registrars, who is charming, and two male doctors, dressed as if they might be going to the pub. What happened to the white coat and stethoscope? My surgeon, the "Picasso of Sinuses", confirms that the surgery has been a success, but he will have to wait for a few days to see if the antibiotics are working. He brings photos of the operation to show me his handiwork, as he usually does. I hang on to them in the hope that one day they might be valuable.

I recall having a colonoscopy (a video of your bowels) a few years ago. As I was leaving the hospital, a man was asking the receptionist whether he could have a copy of the video of the procedure. She looked surprised and went to ask the surgeon. She returned a few minutes later with a DVD.

"Has anyone ever asked for a video of their colonoscopy before?" I asked, after he had left, still somewhat surprised by the request.

"Never," she replied, and we both took a moment to reflect on the idea of visiting a friend's house to see their video of their holiday in Torremolinos followed by his colonoscopy!

"It takes all sorts," she laughed, and I was left wondering whether my friends would be disappointed when I failed to show them mine.

I wonder if there is an internet site for colonoscopy videos. There appears to be one for almost any activity or viewpoint.

10.00am   I talk to a delightful young man in the bed next to me. He is a plumber but became homeless at 16. With help, he worked his way up from living on the streets to a good job. He is an inspirational man.

In the bed opposite is Brian, who is 82 and has an eye problem. He is very distressed about being in the hospital as his wife of 62 years is at home suffering from MS.

The Romanian nurse is efficient and amiable, so I tell her I will learn Romanian. We start with "How are you?" and "Thank you," which I write down. When she returns, I have already forgotten both phrases.

12.00pm   Lunch.

The menu has a byline at the bottom: "The NHS in partnership with Carillion." However, unfortunately, Carillion had already gone into administration.

All my life I have been fascinated by words, phrases, sayings and jokes. I started collecting them at school, so my first book is my fifth form history book – "Peter Bennett. Form 5A. House Tudor. Subject History" – and the first word is "Euchre" which I defined as "An American card game". Second was, strangely, "Celibacy", definition "Abstention (principle)". Why *principle*? But on it went for the last 60 years, with me filling dozens of small notebooks, which I periodically re-read and realise how poor my memory is. I brought some of my notebooks to hospital in the hope that they would cheer me up, but sadly they remained unopened. Feeling particularly low this evening, I opened one and found a couple that cheered me up:

> "What we can laugh at, we can rise above.
> Laughing, we deflect despair.
> Humour is the first cousin of hope."

> "Don't heat the pig to try to make it sing. Much better to sell the pig for bacon and buy a canary."

I shall read a few every day to improve my mood, but also my self-improvement. For example, "Not everything that counts can be counted and not everything that can be counted counts." What good sense!

Reading has always been one of my hobbies, so I start to read one of the books I have brought with me, Elaine Feinstein's *Anna of All the Russians: The Life of Anna Akhmatova*. Anna Akhmatova was born in Ukraine in 1889, became one of Russia's greatest poets and, despite a life of tragedy, persecution and illness, was still capable of sublime, profound and moving poetry. I have always loved her work and keep a portrait of her in my study. Complex but with the heart of a lioness, she showed extraordinary courage in the face of an evil totalitarian regime that tried to destroy her. She would not be silenced and continued to tell "the truth". I was overwhelmed with admiration for a genuinely great (how we overuse that word) individual. One of the outstanding poets of the

20th century, particularly under the circumstances in which she lived.

She produced literature of genius and beauty to reveal to us the eternal truths. There is a poignant story from when she was said to be waiting in a queue outside the Lubyanka prison to hand in a parcel for her son, Lev, who had been sentenced to 10 years in a labour camp, to intimidate her into stopping writing and speaking out. Relatives of those sent to the camps would line up for hours to hand in packages of food and clothing, never knowing whether these items would ever reach their intended beneficiary.

A woman standing next to her recognised her and said, "Can you write about this?"

"I will," replied Akhmatova – and she did, throughout her life, with a courage that shames us in this time of "fake news". She was not allowed to write her poems down, so friends learned them by heart for her, just as, in the camps, Solzhenitsyn had to commit *The Gulag Archipelago* to memory, chapter by chapter, as he had no paper. Had he been discovered he would have been condemned to death. How do these courageous figures find the courage to continue with no assurance that their words will ever be read?

Akhmatova wrote, "That's what my biography is about: who can refuse to live his own life?"

But how many of us do?

Akhmatova answered that question by saying that the talent and power came from God, as did Dostoevsky and Solzhenitsyn, both of whom wrote books of genius under unimaginable circumstances. When she went to Oxford late in her life, in 1968, to receive an honorary degree, she refused to meet the metropolitan bishop of the Russian Orthodox Church in Great Britain. She said, "As a Russian Orthodox Church believer, I would have to tell him the whole truth about the reality in Soviet Russia and I can't." This was because she felt that, as a member of the Church, which did everything the Soviet government required, what she said would get back to the Soviet authorities. (O. S. Guinness, *Long Journey Home*).

After Akhmatova's death, a modern Russian poet said, "When all the politicians who persecuted her, all the police who harassed and tormented her, all those who betrayed her, leaving her to live in poverty and ill health, and those who remained silent when evil took root, are dead and forgotten, the name of Akhmatova will live forever."

And it will.

As Solzhenitsyn said in his Nobel Prize-winning speech, which was read out on his behalf as the authorities would not allow him to travel to receive it:

"One word of truth outweighs the whole world."

That "word of truth" and courage are desperately needed in the relativistic world of lies, corruption, narcissism, cruelty and evil in which we live today.

I don't read for too long as I am exhausted after the operation. Hopefully, I will get some sleep between getting my IV three times a day, 6am, 2pm and 10pm.

I dwell on what Akhmatova wrote in her diary: "After a lengthy stay, all hospitals turn into prisons."

"Every day I think about dying, illness, disease
starvation, violence, the end of the world. It
helps me keep my mind off things."
Roger McGough

4

Childhood and Primary School

I t is strange how powerfully my lying in bed, exhausted and unable to concentrate, causes long-forgotten memories to be revived even so soon after my admission.

As far as I can recall, I was a happy, large, but challenging child, one who would throw a tantrum if I did not get what I wanted. My mother would tell the story of taking me shopping in my pram, letting me loose to get some exercise until, having been denied my chosen confectionery, I would plummet to the floor, yelling at the appalling child neglect. Annoyingly I didn't have a mobile phone back in 1948 and Esther Rantzen had not yet started her "Helpline", so my only recourse was to make as much noise as a three-year-old's lungs were capable of producing. My mother was not made for heavy lifting work, so it would require the help of a couple of sturdy shop assistants or fellow shoppers to get me back into my pram, secured in a way that would test Harry Houdini. By the time we got home, I would have calmed down and, being someone who has never borne a grudge, our mutual adoration was restored.

My second notable parental challenge was that I would never go to sleep. Luckily, one of our neighbours was a direct descendant of the Goddess of Sleep and so would be called upon to exert her mystical powers in order to induce my gentle slumber. As I got older, I noted that she was a heavy drinker and so I started to wonder whether her powers were in fact more medicinal than divine.

I started primary school in September 1951, aged six. There I met my oldest friend, Robert ("Crusty" – nobody knows why!?) Stephens. He wrote to me in September 2021 to acknowledge 70 years of friendship. I replied, recognizing that we had never had a row. How many couples can say that? Anyway, more of him later. The headmaster was a tall, imposing man, Mr Snowden. Although I passed the 11+ early, due to my birth date, I could not go on to the local grammar school and had to wait another year at primary school. So, to Mr Snowden's frustration, he was left with me for a year with nothing to do – much as was the case in the hospital bed. I played a lot of football with Mr Ashbridge, a brilliant footballer, teacher and mentor. Otherwise, Mr Snowden had to find projects to keep me occupied. His first such was to have me spend a month recording the number plates of cars passing the school, which proved rather stressful because the road was a busy dual carriageway.

Next, as we were adjacent to a golf course and he played, I had to go and find as many balls as possible. I don't think that Mr Snowden ever had to buy a golf ball again. It was a public course, and I met many interesting people. It also initiated my love of golf.

One chap I met regularly was a man who carried his clubs in a pram, accompanied by a baby. He taught me some of golf's greatest lessons, for example: how to play a bunker shot when a 16-month-old boy is yelling his head off. During my golfing career, I have, therefore, never had a problem with crowd noise. In fact, of course, this has never been tested as I have never played in front of a crowd aside from the rabbits on the 17th hole of my local golf course who are, I have to admit, exceptionally well behaved as golf fans tend to be. I never hear a rabbit yell "You're the man!" after a particularly (rare!) reasonable tee shot.

In despair, Mr Snowden instructed me to study the stars, and, after a few months, I knew every star in the sky and developed insomnia. In the years long before OFSTED, nobody realised the effect on a 10-year-old boy of having no sleep.

At last, in desperation, and with no real hope of success, Mr Snowden decided to enter me for a scholarship to the local public school. This would require me to undertake some academic work and relieved him of the pressure of finding me another project.

The exam took place on a Saturday in an environment consistent with a privileged, expensive education: imposing Victorian buildings set in beautiful surroundings with top-class rugby pitches and cricket nets and squares. I recall feeling that I had not completely embarrassed myself in the morning written papers. However, the afternoon test was of general knowledge, combined with a test of one's ability to describe articulately a range of objects which were laid out on a large table. These included, as far as I can remember, a radio, a piece of coal, a turtle shell, a stuffed bird, a brick, a thermometer and many others beside.

Unfortunately, the elderly master supervising this part of the exam had obviously had throat surgery and didn't speak through his mouth, but through a hole in his throat, covered in a fine mesh. He sounded like a drunken Dalek, and I couldn't understand a word he said. The idea was that he would announce an object that I had to pick up and describe to him. I was too young and nervous to ask for clarification. So, when a word came whistling through the mesh, it was lucky dip time for me. The only clue to aid me with my lack of paranormal intelligence was when he emitted a strange disapproving strangling sound, rather like a bird caught in a trap. I recall hearing what I thought was the word "telescope" and fortunately, with enormous relief, following my recent project on the stars, was able to provide a detailed account of the history and mechanics of the instrument. The master responded by reproducing what appeared to be the tragic, final moments of the bird in the trap. On reflection, this was his way of conveying the message, "Put the bloody thing down! I said *thermometer*."

Mr Snowden called me in a few weeks later to say, "Good news and bad news, Bennett. You did rather well in the written papers, but they are concerned that they were not told about your disability."

"Disability?" I replied.

"Deafness," he said. "Which, I have to say, I hadn't noticed. When the master announced the microscope, you picked up and described the stuffed bird, and when the piece of coal was announced, you described the radio and so on. However, they have taken a sympathetic view and offered you a half-scholarship on the basis that you will accept help from the local deaf school."

For whatever reason, probably financial, my parents did me a huge favour by not accepting the offer. Instead, I went to Waterloo Grammar.

"Child psychologists generally do a good job, but I find they are more helpful once they're a bit older."

5

The Bed, the Light, the Noise
(and the TV System)

6 am and I am beyond tired. Sleep experts tell us that the essentials for restful, energizing sleep are a good bed, and a quiet, dark environment. Sadly, none of these seems to apply in this ward. I was thrust into the hospital day at 6am, having had no sleep.

The Bed

The temperature in the ward is tropical, and the windows don't open. The mattress is covered in a plastic/rubber compound, which is slippery. The bottom sheets are too small for the mattress and so have no chance of staying in place. The top sheet is also too small, as is the blanket, so cannot be tucked under the mattress to secure them for the night. The pillowcase is too large for the pillow and, more importantly, does not have a "tuck" at the open end to keep the pillow in situ overnight. The pillow is, again, made of a rubbery material which, through age, has lost its smoothness and has been transformed into a hard, corrugated surface.

You wake in the morning sweating and swaddled in the sheets to the point of mummification. The rubbery pillow has reached boiling point and has either escaped to a cooler climate on the floor, or gets stuck halfway out, so you have spent the night risking facial burns from the hot, corrugated rubber. Therefore, during the night, you either strangle yourself, drown in your own sweat, or require plastic surgery.

The Light

At one end of the ward is a large window with French blinds which have, unfortunately, been broken and not repaired. I am next to the window, so my bed is illuminated by the bright fluorescent lights from the nearby hospital buildings.

Do all of them have to be kept on all night?

At the other end of the ward is a window in the door leading on to the corridor. It is so bright that it is possible to read during the night without turning the ward light on.

The Noise

During my stay, I had at least one fellow inmate with sleep apnoea whose snoring constituted a pretty decent impersonation of a steam train but was not conducive to a good night's sleep. Also, a brain-damaged Liverpool drug addict who spent the night crying out his various complaints – with every other word being an expletive.

So, my initial thoughts/suggestions on sleep deprivation as a new boy:

1. Get the Secretary of State for Health and the chief executive of the local NHS trust to live and sleep on the ward for a week and see if they are capable of undertaking gainful employment thereafter. Or, add in a number of "celebrities" and have a hospital version of *I'm a Celebrity, Get Me out of Here*. I think this would test even Harry Redknapp!

2. They have two types of bed. The majority of patients stay in hospital for a few days – e.g. hip replacements, and so the shortage of sleep does not impact too negatively on their recovery. However, the longer-stay patients should have a more comfortable, modern bed, as a good night's sleep is one of the essential elements for a successful and speedy recovery.

3. As on aeroplanes, distribute earplugs.

A decent bed, darkness, and as quiet environment as possible may help the healing process.

And while I am here, two further suggestions occurred to me:

4. A different buzzer. If I press the red buzzer, the nurse does not know whether I am about to shuffle off this mortal coil or just want a coffee and a couple of digestive biscuits. So, I thought, why not have a red one for medical needs and a blue one for snacks to avoid the nurse arriving, puffing and panting, to undertake artificial respiration on a patient who just wants a custard cream. When I put it to her, the idea was undermined by a nurse who pointed out that a confused patient could just as easily press blue and be dead when the coffee and biscuits arrived.

5. Nurses should carry a little pad to record any requests by patients as so many seem to be forgotten, presumably because they are busy and distracted by other patients' requests. They are like waiters in pretentious restaurants who, rather than writing your order down, pretend to remember it, which invariably means you get the wrong dish.

The staff today are Polish, Czech, Italian, Spanish, Romanian and Indian. Have given up my idea of learning "Good morning," "How are you?", and "Thank you," in each language, having failed after 100 attempts to learn them in Romanian. Then remembered that I was bottom of the class in French for five consecutive years at school, so I have to conclude that I just have no natural talent for languages.

A lovely Polish lady brings me my breakfast. She looks

rather depressed, but when she smiles, she has the most beautiful expression and seems to lighten up. She wears one of those very unflattering statutory "Health and Safety" caps that covers her hair. She looks about 35 but tells me that she is a grandmother with a three-year-old granddaughter.

The personalities of the nurses seem to reflect their nationality, ranging from the more extrovert Italians to the gentle, more reserved Indian nurses.

One nurse, in particular, stands out. She is Romanian and has the look of an angel. Some of the nurses complain about certain patients' behaviour, but she just says, angelically: "Everyone has their problems."

I think about how tough it must be to leave your home (most of them are unmarried), in, say, Kerala, and travel from a warm Indian climate to a damp, cold English winter's day. The trust has, apparently, recruited 25 Indian nurses, but only two have arrived. One of them tells me that in India they are taught English, but also speak a local language at home, while the national language is Hindi. They do seem to be thrown in at the deep end on arrival, which can cause some language problems. However, I suspect that this is not their fault.

One of the Italian nurses is very funny and tells me that she loves the cinema. I am a bit of a film buff, and we agree that the Italians have made some of the greatest films in history. I tell her that my favourite is *Cinema Paradiso*, written and directed by Giuseppe Tornatore. She agrees but has only seen the shorter version which won the Oscar for Best Foreign Film in 1985. The original version, the

Director's Cut, had been shortened because they felt it was simply too long for the American attention span. The Director's Cut is an infinitely better film, one that makes me weep every time I see it.

There is, however, one nurse (male) who worries me. He prowls the ward with the look of a man with anger management issues and is fighting back the urge to slaughter anyone within 20 yards. Thank God for British gun laws.

I am beginning to work out the nursing hierarchy:

- Dark blue uniform: senior nurse – probably ward sister.
- White with blue banding: fully trained nurse, capable of, for example, putting in a cannula.
- White: junior nurse – restricted to minor tasks.
- Light blue: assistant – answers your red buzzer and determines whether you want a snack (which they get for you, if they remember) or tells a more senior nurse if it is a medical problem.
- Student nurses – doing a three-year degree at the local university. These student nurses do 700 hours a year in the hospital with a trained mentor.

My initial assessment of nurses is as follows, and it probably applies to most occupations, certainly the legal profession in which I practised for 30 years. Out of every ten nurses, I would suggest that:

- Two are born to it, naturals – for example, the Romanian nurse.

- Six are potentially very good, given the right training, mentoring and environment.
- Two are totally unsuited to the profession.

A problem appears to be that getting rid of the latter two is impossible and would presumably exacerbate the recruitment crisis. How expensive is it to send a recruitment team to Kerala?

One of two unsuited ones sits permanently outside the ward, hunched over a computer. She never smiles and looks suspiciously as if she could be ex-KGB.

11.00am   I call a nurse because the cannula in my hand coming loose. A young nurse tries to change it, without success, and tells me she will get another nurse.

One thing that surprises me already is the shortage of senior nurses. In my experience in the private sector, there are a lot of nurses with 20-30 years of experience. Here, there appears to be only one.

"Why?" I ask the nurses.

The overwhelming response is the "appalling management" which seems to be a major demotivating factor. They speak of a fear of the management who disagree with their views and do not appear on the wards. I ask a nurse whether the management ever do a night shift.

"No!"

If I remember correctly, Jeremy Hunt, when Secretary

of State for Health, worked in a hospital one day a week. The question I have it, for how long and what did he do? Talk to the patients? Clean the ward? Serve lunches? One nurse said, "Of course all the senior management have private health insurance."

Some 18 of the 20 nurses on the ward are foreign and relatively young. A Spanish nurse tells me that he has doubled his salary by coming to the UK, and if he gets a good hospital on his CV, he can return home and earn more, for example, in a private hospital. I was told that in Spain the unemployment rate following the 2008 financial crisis has been very high. It was reported that at a nursing college in Andalusia only two out of 100 graduated nurses had managed to find a job in Spain. The salaries are also very low. Therefore, the nurses come to the UK where there are more jobs, and the salary is considerably higher. This appears to coincide with the number of training UK nurses falling.

As I lie in bed, I muse on what proportion of nursing should be related to technical skills, and what percentage empathy and compassion. 50-50? 70-30? 40-60? Compassion for the patient is vitally important and does seem to be in short supply. Why? Are the nurses too busy? Is the ward understaffed? Although, if I go for a walk, there are often two or three nurses at the nurses' desk, chatting or looking at their mobile phones. Should there not be a discipline whereby, if you are not busy, you go and talk to the patients, listen to their stories, some of which will be remarkable records of achievements to inspire or emulate? Or just comfort them? I am coming to realise that this missing element has a significant impact on how you feel. The hospital day is long, noisy, uncomfortable and stressful. This is in contrast to the private sector where you are in a single room, and the nurses appear every so often to see how you are and to have a chat. I recall being in a private room for over a month with septic arthritis, and although my wife visited every day, I would become very tearful at night. A nurse would come, sit and hold my hand. Sometimes for 30 minutes. It was a real lifesaver.

Brian is in the bed opposite me. He is 86 and has been married for 62 years. He lives at home and looks after his wife who has multiple sclerosis. He has an eye condition. He is very lonely and depressed, and the nurses think he is getting confused. He is nothing of the sort, I learn when I go and chat with him over coffee and biscuits; he is just very distressed and emotional. He occasionally speaks on the phone, but it is the stress that is causing his confusion, and NOT any medical condition. He is a really lovely man. His son is a radiologist in the United States, and "earns a fortune". He and his wife used to visit a lot but cannot do so anymore. What I find confusing is that, other than giving him his eye drops, none of the nurses comes and chats to him or holds his hand. Every time they come, I shout over, "Do you know he has been married for 62 years?"

Nobody seemed interested in knowing.

"After two days in hospital I took a turn for the nurse."
W.C. Fields

6

More Thoughts and Experiences
from Day Three

Although I am desperately tired, my mood is lifted when the Romanian nurse greets me in the corridor with a huge smile, one that would light up one of Stephen Hawking's black holes. She always smiles. She squeezes my hand and asks how I am. She is the embodiment of nursing.

11.30am   I am very concerned about Brian.

Brian is more and more like a wilting flower. He lies on his bed, seemingly getting ever smaller and sadder. Outside the ward, four nurses stand talking. Nobody goes to talk to him except a very good Spanish nurse who gives him a hug when administering his eye drops. He deserves better treatment. I continue to get him coffee and give him chocolate biscuits that my daughter brought me. She goes and has a chat with him on her visits, and he says to me afterwards, "Isn't she wonderful? So kind!"

Why is this happening? In the US, I believe, they have so called "Hospital Angels" who visit patients. It seems simple, but they don't appear to have them in this hospital.

12.00am	Still no sign of the cannula change. Lunch: fishcakes and vegetables, which are overcooked. On a blind testing, it would be difficult to tell the difference between a sprout and a carrot. Pie without custard. So dry.
12.50pm	I ask the nurse again if my cannula can be changed. She calls the KGB officer from her seat outside the ward, who changes it with the ruthless efficiency you would expect. No smile, no small talk or apology for her colleagues' failed attempts. Returns to her computer station.
1.30pm	Thinking about lunch and the catering. Contracted out! Would love to see the sub-contractor contracts.

Rather disgruntled after two days in bed, I go for a walk and discover the patients' sitting room, which is full of people waiting to be admitted or discharged from eye surgery. There is a framed poem tucked away behind the curtain:

When we are well, we see nothing,
We hurry throughout the day,
We rush from one thing to another.

No time to smell the roses and play.
Why is it that when we feel poorly,
Confined perhaps to our bed,
We see a different perspective,
Of the road on which we are led?
We begin to value a kindness,
Our world starts to settle and still,
Have we really gained an advantage?
And appreciate more when we're ill.
Try to look at this time of progression,
Of spirit and you'll find on the whole,
The body responds to upliftment,
Making good health your positive goal.

Lynn New

How many people see it, never mind read it? Why not put it in each ward? The walls of the hospital are festooned with expensive posters encouraging us to lose weight, give up smoking, clean our hands properly, teaching us how to spot the symptoms of meningitis or dengue fever, which nobody appears to read. There is one particularly large poster on good quality paper. It shows a pair of hands in handcuffs, warning us that abuse of staff can lead to a prison sentence. I ask a nurse, who has worked in the hospital for some years, if it ever happened.

"No," she replies, and tells me that the only physical problems they encounter are the involuntary actions of patients with, for example, dementia or drunks/drug addicts who presumably can't read or remember the poster anyway.

There is another poster of "Night-time promises".

The Night-time Promises

There are promises prominently displayed around the hospital.

We promise to ensure that you:

1. Are as comfortable as possible.
2. Have everything you need, such as an extra blanket.
3. Don't disturb others and that others don't disturb you – e.g. switching off your TV or use a headphone.

And we promise to ensure that we:

1. Keep our voices and any other noise to a minimum.
2. Turn off or soften any bright lights.
3. Use pen torches when making checks during the nights.
4. Turn the volume down on telephones or equipment.
5. Promptly respond to and switch off any buzzers or alarms.
6. Avoid overnight bed moves by planning ahead.
7. Only disturb you if absolutely necessary.

If you feel that these promises have not been met, please ask to speak to the ward manager.

Signed Role:	Ward Sister
Ward name	Date

These are PROMISES. A definition of a promise is, "A declaration or assurance that one will do something or that a particular thing will happen." So, I must ask myself, are the bed, the noise, the light all broken promises? Or do they subscribe to the view of Jonathan Swift that promises and piecrusts are made to be broken?"

I note that there is no promise of a bed that you can sleep in, curtains to provide darkness, or not having a 6' 5" brain-damaged drug addict yelling all night, "No fuckin' Weetabix, fuckin' telly doesn't work, this place is crap!" I never saw a pen torch so presume they had been part of the latest round of cuts.

Another quirk that puzzled me as I lay in that uncomfortable bed was why some hospitals had expensive art collections on the walls? Art that mostly nobody looks at, and if they do, they can't make out what it is because of postmodern abstraction. It is a *hospital*, not an *art gallery*! Just get schoolchildren to paint the walls with happy faces, I think, and you will have solved the problem and saved money. I heard that a hospital in London employs an art curator.

A large whiteboard, prominently displayed on the wall where we cannot miss it, records the performance of the ward SSIP, The Specialist Surgery Inpatient Ward Quality and Safety Board. The board has two sections, patient experience and staffing. There is nothing in the staffing column. The patient experience column is 92%, and that is the percentage of patients who have said that they are extremely likely or likely to recommend the hospital. Under the patient safety column, there is a list of expectations, all of which seem to be close to 100%.

The interesting thing about the statistics is that they are all compiled by the members of staff. It would appear unusual if the figure did not show a decent performance.

In the Trust Annual Report, much is made of the Patient Satisfaction Survey. Interestingly, I was never asked to complete one and nor was any patient I talked to. I imagine that most people are so glad to get out that they would not give a thought to whether they would "recommend the services to family or friends," who would, in any case, have no choice of hospitals were they, sadly, to need to be admitted.

Lying in bed for hours with little to do, my mind pondered questions for which I had no answer – is there an independent body that audits the figures before they are presented to the public? How are they calculated? Is, for example, the percentage of satisfied patients based on the number who completed the form, or the total number of patients admitted to the hospital during the year? Obviously, the results would be very different. From my, admittedly limited, experience, I suspect that only a few patients even completed the form.

Presumably, there is a bonus scheme for the smallest number of biscuits handed out. I ask the trolley man if he could take away my old cup. He looks shocked and says, "No, I only do deliveries. Pick-up is different."

I have noticed that none of the catering staff smiles.

In the evening, the first comedy act appears. A very large

chap with a broad Brummie accent arrives and tells us all, very loudly, that his son is having surgery, and he is waiting for him to return to the ward. As he prowls around, he loudly complains that he is gagging for a pint but, believe it or not, the hospital doesn't have a bar.

"Can you fuckin' believe it?" he asks, and concludes, "They'd make a fortune, calming me nerves."

Eventually, his son returns to his allotted bed.

"'Ow's mum?" he asks.

"She kicked me out," replies the father. "Says it was my fault you got pissed and fell over. Anyway, get some kip, lad. I'm gagging for a pint."

At about 8 the following morning, Dad arrives to take his son home. Dad is soaking wet.

"'Ow did you get on last night?" the son asks.

"Rang your mum," Dad replies, "but she told me the door was locked, 'so don't think about coming home.' So I went to a pub nearby. Had a few bevvies and slept in A+E. Couldn't get a wink because of the drunks and druggies coming in! And you know what? The heartless bastards kicked me out at 6 in the morning and it's pissing down."

They left together an hour later with Dad still complaining about the lack of a bar. Sadly, I don't know if marital harmony was restored.

Around 4pm a new patient arrives in the bed to my left, screened off as we are by a thin curtain. Some wards like ours have only six beds, which are about four feet apart. We are told that it creates a therapeutic ambience as it allows the patients to share their pain and problems. The thing is that nobody talks, except when they are on the phone or talking to the staff, and then we are all listening in.

Later in the evening, there is a loud commotion in the corridor which I go to investigate. There are four young heavyweight men, wearing black military-style outfits. I gather that there is a large drug scene in the city, which is dominated by two rival gangs who have decided to fight it out for supremacy. One gang leader made a positive statement of intent by attempting to behead his rival. Sadly, he had missed his recent appointment at Specsavers and had only managed to remove half. The patient, bleeding profusely, was taken off to surgery. The men in black are police officers from the drugs squad. They, the doctors and nurses should receive medals along with our recognition and thanks.

With little distraction, one's senses are sharpened, and I find that lying all day with almost nothing to do, I begin to notice much more detail than ever before. For example, I notice that the police equipment includes a very impressive mobile phone. The sight of this sets me off on one of my pet grouses in life – why do people use their phones so much, especially in public spaces such as on the train? I have always considered this discourteous. Why should I be forced to listen to the tedious details of other people's lives? Mine is tedious enough as it is. Although occasionally you do get to eavesdrop on what I call "blackmail material". Once, I was on a train when the man sitting opposite rang and said, lovingly, to the person on the other end, "I'm so sorry, darling, having another late night. Won't be back until after 12. Kiss the kids good night for me." He immediately redialled, and this time it was, "Darling, be with you at 7. Love you." Why don't they just text? Sadly, I haven't seen the man since to arrange where the money should be left.

My mind, having taken me from the police to trains, via the mobile phone, I now suddenly recall the best announcement I ever heard on a train. I was travelling from London to Liverpool, and we stopped, unannounced at Watford. The Tannoy clicked on and someone with a Liverpool accent told us, "Good evening, ladies and gentlemen, on this the 5.45 to Liverpool. Unfortunately, due to a stray hippo on the line, we shall be delayed for approximately 30 minutes at Watford." We all looked at each other in bemusement, but the announcer continued, having clearly forgotten to turn off the Tannoy, "That'll keep the bastards quiet." There followed a brief pause and then we heard, "Oh fuck! I've left the mic on."

I imagine that he now has a senior management role with one of the major rail franchises.

"That which thou hast promised must thou perform."
Brothers Grimm

7

Death's Waiting Room – Daily Reflections (and the Medical Staff)

Day Four – Sunday 4th November, 2019

6.00am   Asked a nurse if she could get me a pair of socks, sheets and towels. She said she would ask someone to get them.

A Nigerian-born nurse introduces herself to me. Her name is difficult to pronounce, and I say that I understand that Nigerian names have meanings, for example, my local chemist is named Tolofu, which means "Walking with God". She says her name means "Walking with Wealth". I ask her if it has worked.

"Not so far," she says, laughing.

7.00am   In the paper I read, "Church warden and magician arrested in murder inquiry." What was the inspiration behind it, I wonder? Anyway, the body might rise from the dead or disappear, saving police time and money.

It reminded me of my life in the newspaper industry and some of the adverts placed in the For Sale section:

1: "Used tombstone. Would suit family named Anderson."

2: "Geordie, although 6, is friendly, well-trained and loving. Loves long walks and chocolate biscuits. Would live with another dog after formal introduction. Will not live in Luton." Why not Luton? Had the dog been a Luton Town FC supporter who had become disillusioned after recent performances?

7.30am   Ask the nurse at the desk about the socks, sheets and towel. She is looking at her phone, presumably doing some medical research which I am reluctant to halt. She tells me she will get someone to get them and make the bed.

8.30am   Nothing has happened, but I discover that the cabinet containing stocks of socks, towels and sheets is at the end of my bed. I get them and make the bed. Thirty minutes later, a new nurse arrives to take my blood pressure and heart rate. The machine goes berserk, flashing lights and buzzing. I start sweating profusely, death appears to be imminent. "What is wrong?" she asks

"I've just spent 30 minutes making the bloody bed."

For the first time I feel trapped. I can't go out and my life is controlled by others. I get the feeling that conformity is required, and I am reminded of my late father-in-law, a fiery Welshman, who decided that conformity could have unacceptable consequences. He was admitted to hospital aged about 75, much against his will, as his self-diagnosis showed him to be in perfect condition. In a ward of elderly patients, he noticed that a patient was moved to the bed by the door at night but was not there in the morning. He wondered what was happening. Was this death's waiting room? Was the Grim Reaper the ticket-collector? One night they moved him to the bed by the door. He was not ready to meet the Angel of Death, so at 2am he got up, in his pyjamas, ordered a taxi and went home. As he told me early the next morning, while tucking into a hearty breakfast, "No way was I going to die."

He never went back.

I have become obsessed with President Trump's inability to tell the truth and its potentially dangerous consequences, some of which we have seen during the Covid 19 pandemic when he proved incapable of even telling the truth.

Although unable to predict the way his lies would be a matter of life and death for so many, I spend my time reading more in the paper about the world of Trumpian make-believe. How can 63 million people believe a malignant narcissist who lies about 10 times a day? The Greeks believed that democracy was potentially self-destructive because a strong, persuasive demagogue can lead vast numbers of people down the road to barbarism – as the 20th century showed so catastrophically. However, now we have the power to destroy the world. As Viktor Frankl said, "Since Auschwitz we know what man is capable of. And since Hiroshima we know what is at stake." Evil must be recognized for what it is and obliterated with all the force at our disposal.

I recall that W.H. Auden, who moved to America during the second world war, experienced the reality of evil when watching a film about the Holocaust and hearing the audience's brutal responses. He wrote, "Suddenly I saw the existence of Evil as a reality. All I have is a voice to unfold the folded lie." He realised that life was not relativistic, but there were absolutes which were being undermined.

According to O.S. Guinness's *The Long Journey Home*, Auden summed it up:

Either we serve the unconditional
Or some Hitlerian monster will supply
An iron conviction to do evil by.

It has been a quiet day. Only one admission as far as I can see. Several nurses are sitting together at the nurse's station, looking at their telephones or computers. Hospital days are long and lonely, and I am very tired because of lack of sleep, so reading becomes difficult. I try to relax but find it hard. How strange it is that in such unusual surroundings, memories are revived which life's constant trivial distractions had caused me to forget.

11.00am   A young consultant arrives, aged about 40, dressed expensively – smart casual for a Sunday morning shift. He is obviously very bright with the self-confident air of a man who has risen quickly through the ranks, giving rise to a suggestion of arrogance. He doesn't introduce himself or the young female doctor accompanying him who is pushing a large computer system held on a waist-high stand.

The junior doctor is very tall, slightly stooped with an aquiline nose. She reminds me of a young Edith Sitwell, and like Sitwell her academic austerity causes the temperature in the room to fall a few degrees. Her job appears to be to record on the computer her boss's words of wisdom. She is a latter-day medical biographer, like James Boswell to his friend and contemporary Samuel Johnson, described by the *Oxford Dictionary of National Biography* as "arguably the most distinguished man of letters in British history." As Boswell's volume was only 422 pages long it is obvious that he did not recall everything that Johnson wrote, but applied some judicious editorial discernment. Today, Edith decides that there is nothing momentous enough to preserve for future historians and remains inactive.

In order to remain active and ward off the Grim

Reaper, I point to the computer and say, "Presumably, this is the Chariot of Life." Well, I might as well have sung the Nepalese national anthem, and my limited attempt at humour falls on deaf ears.

As he is about to leave, I delay him by telling him that I have a couple of rare neurological conditions and would like his help. He turns back and looks as if Homer Simpson has spoken.

"Have you heard of Propriospinal Myoclonus and Idiopathic Hypersomnia?" I ask politely.

He hesitates momentarily, caught between revealing an intellectual weakness or denying that he hasn't. His eyes turn to Edith Sitwell, but she is obviously working on a new sonnet.

"No, but what has it got to do with your condition?" he says, looking bored.

I explain the problem of the bed and being unable to sleep, which adversely affects the problem.

"Couldn't agree more," he says, "used to sleep on them when I was a junior doctor, absolutely impossible. The only problem is that it is the only bed we have. Could your family bring in some sheets, pillows and a duvet?"

"What about a bed?" I ask ironically.

"Not sure the management would allow that," he replies earnestly.

With that, he turns to leave, taking Edith by surprise and bumping into her and the Chariot, causing them to ride out of the ward together like a couple of lovers on a scooter. I imagine his post-lunch reading will be *Otolaryngology Monthly*.

11.30am   Go for a walk before lunch. I come across Edith
             Sitwell crouched over the computer chariot. As
             we are now in a doctor/patient relationship,
             I say, "Hello." Not a flicker of recognition.
             Obviously, she had made a greater impression
             on me than I on her. Maybe I am not seen as
             a person but as a medical condition – Frontal
             Sinuses – or a bed – SSIP 28C.

Suddenly, thought, it was obvious. I had missed a brilliant
new NHS plan. Build "Android Doctors" whose memory
banks contain all human medical knowledge and can
be updated periodically. So, sitting at the computer, was
she being upgraded? Think of the announcement in
Parliament! "No more foreign doctors and 5000 more
doctors have been recruited immediately at no further
cost!" A vote winner!

12.00pm   Lunch – turkey breast slices with unidentifiable
             vegetables and the smallest tub of ice cream I
             have ever seen.

There is a notice on the menu about hand hygiene which
reads, "The trust takes it very seriously." *Unlike cleaning
the ward and toilets,* I think as I read it.

3.00pm   Finish the Akhmatova biography.

My mind drifts back to the idea of Solzhenitsyn's "One
word of truth outweighs the whole world" at a time when

a senior White House official can with a straight face talk about "alternative facts" and recognise with alarm that we are in a really dark place – the recent impeachment inquiry in Congress has shown just how dark it is. It is said that George Washington could not tell a lie, and that Richard Nixon could not tell the truth, and now we have Donald Trump who doesn't know the difference between the two.

Some secular and religious leaders who have lost all sense of morality in pursuit of power and money will be judged harshly by posterity and, if you read Dante's *Divine Comedy*, will have plenty of time to discuss their cowardice in his circles of hell.

As H.L. Mencken wrote so presciently more than a century ago, "On some great and glorious day, the plain folks of the land will reach their heart's desire at last, and the White House will be adorned by a moron."

The question I ask myself is, is this a new phenomenon? Have we evolved the "selfish gene" to the point where we suffer from profound amnesia? No, I don't believe that this is the case, for as the Greek playwright Aristophanes wrote c. 400 BC, "Politics these days is no occupation for an educated man. Ignorance and lousiness are better for a politician who must be neither educated nor honest. He must be an ignoramus or a rogue."

Why do we never learn the lessons of history? History has always provided us with inspirational writers and leaders who remind us of the truth. Coincidentally, I recently read a book, *Heroic Leadership* by Chris Lowney (Loyola Press), in which I was reminded of the work of the Jesuit movement, found and inspired by St Ignatius Loyola (1491-1556). It engendered four unique values which seem sensible to me:

- Self-awareness
- Ingenuity
- Love
- Heroism

The Jesuits equipped their members to succeed by modelling themselves on a leader who:

- Understood their strengths, weaknesses, values and world view.
- Confidently innovated and adapted to embrace a changing world.
- Engaged others with a positive, loving attitude.

He taught his followers to:

- Energise themselves and others through heroic ambition in a bottom-up system of leadership, leaders and managers.
- Lead by inspiring others through their own example, creating environments of greater love than fear.
- Find and develop *altissimo* (the highest and best).
- Help subordinates locate their inner switch for motivational performance.
- Trust and support those who are on the ground.

Do we have such leaders in business, politics or in the NHS? Great leaders inspire the individual to think of "we" and not "I"? As J.F. Kennedy said in his inaugural speech, "Ask not what your country can do for you, ask what you can do for your country." If a society does not, or cannot, have the shared values of justice, freedom of speech, and the rule of law, some leaders will embrace the latest popular fad which inevitably leads to totalitarian repression. This is put well in Linda Grant's introduction to the great 20th century novel, *Life and Fate*, by Vasily Grossman: "All that matters is the individual, and the furious joy of being alive as human beings and to die as human beings. Not as the mouthpieces of unreality."

There is a new male Italian nurse on the ward, and he has come to change the cannula on the back of my hand. He is very intense and rather opinionated. Obviously been to the Mussolini school of nursing as he expects everyone to do as he tells them, particularly the patients. However, bless him, he produces the answer to the cannula problem – put it in the arm, leaving the hand free. Why doesn't anyone else do it like that? It seems so simple. Do they have group meetings to discuss potential improvements?

Each student has a senior nurse to mentor them, and the Italian nurse is mentoring O, a fascinating third-year student, aged about 35 and unmarried. O was a professional footballer in Germany but had to retire due to a leg injury. He looks very strong and must weigh about 80 kg. He tells me his hobby is arm-wrestling, which I had never heard of as a sport before. My only experience is being in the pub as a student after a few pints, pitted against a small, 5' 6" man weighing about 10 stone, who would bend the arm of my 6' 3", 14-stone frame within seconds, while singing the Beatles' "Let It Be". I comfort myself talking to O, that my humiliating defeat was probably due to a lack of technique. He tells me that nowadays it's a bona fide sport with organized tournaments and has been since the 1950s. In fact, O has just returned from the European Arm-Wrestling Championships. How on earth, after being a sports fanatic for 74 years, have I missed this one? O explains the various techniques involved and seems keen to demonstrate them on me. Remembering my poor track record, I feign injury to avoid having a plaster cast on my arm as well as two holes in my head.

Poor Brian opposite is desperate for human contact and deeply depressed as no one ever visits him. I often go over and talk to him, get him a coffee, provide more chocolate biscuits, and listen to him talk about his fascinating life. I ask him the secret of being married for 62 years.

"Don't say a lot," he replies.

9.24pm   The elderly man in the bed opposite had plastic surgery earlier today. He was sleeping peacefully when a doctor woke him up and said that her department was doing a questionnaire, and would he be so kind as to complete it.

"Now?!" he replied sleepily.

"OK, any time before you leave," she replied.

I suspect my answer to her might have been rather less polite. Why doesn't someone come and ask him when he is feeling better… and awake?

"It's not that I'm afraid of dying. I just don't want to be there when it happens."
Woody Allen

8

Nepal, Brian Goes Home (and My New, Heroic Neighbour)

Day Five – Monday 5th November, 2018

6.00am   Slept badly again. Went back to sleep, and Brian kindly ordered my breakfast.

7.00am   Woken by a charming new nurse. She is Nepalese, the first Nepalese person I have ever met. I know nothing about the country, other than it has very high mountains. So, I looked it up on Wikipedia. It has a population of 26.4 million. It is the 48th largest country by population and the 93rd by area. It has China to the north, India to the south, and Bangladesh 17 miles from the south-eastern tip. Bhutan is separated from it by the Indian state of

Sikkim. The capital is Kathmandu, and it is the home of the world's highest mountain, Mount Everest. Its motto is, "Mother and motherland are greater than heaven." The national anthem is "Made of Hundreds of Flowers". It has six regional languages but, surprisingly, legal documents are written in English.

The nurse's grandfather was a Gurkha, and she came to England with her parents as a child. She was educated in the UK and speaks perfect English. She got three A level and trained at University College London and then at the Neurological Hospital in London. Obviously, she is destined for great things.

For some reason, as I think about Nepal, I remember the Beatles' album *Magical Mystery Tour* and adapt some of the songs for life in hospital.

"Fool on the Hill" becomes "Fool on the Bed" who knew absolutely nothing about Nepal.

"Hello Goodbye" – doctors' rather quick visits.

"All You Need Is Love" – the whole organization.

9.00am My brilliant surgeon arrives with his team. He has a wonderful female registrar and two junior doctors. My surgeon is his usual positive, charming self. Even though the news is not good (more blood tests – with results,

77

hopefully, on Saturday), I feel good for seeing them.

Brian is being discharged, thank God. The loneliness and sadness are killing him.

After lunch, I start thinking about the cleaning operation in the hospital which, I learn, has been contracted out. Today, the toilets have not been cleaned again. The hospital's laziness/incompetence award can be won comfortably by the man who is supposed (I imagine) to clean our ward. He is idle, bored, sullen and seemingly blind. He brightens the room by leaving it. He positively radiates gloom.

3.00pm   Brian is still here.

Brian has been dressed and waiting to leave for over three hours. Getting very distressed about his niece picking him up. I go over and chat with him. We share a coffee and another pack of chocolate biscuits.

She finally arrives, and as he leaves, I give him a couple of packets of biscuits to take home. Brian thanks me and says, tearfully, "You know, you are the only thing that has kept me going."

I reply (also tearfully), "Many thanks. It has been one of the things that has kept me going."

We shake hands, and I ask him to let me know how he is getting on. An outstanding man. I pray that life goes well for him and his wife.

The man in the next bed, who is Czech, is about 50 and came into the hospital a month ago for routine foot surgery. Unfortunately, he has developed a serious infection and has lost a lot of the skin on his foot. He says that when they took the bandages off, all he could see was a collection of bones. The plastic surgeon who visits him is brisk and to the point and leaves him without allowing him to ask any questions, which he finds frustrating. I am initially critical, but then think of the sights a hospital plastic surgeon must see.

My new neighbour is genuinely heroic and recommends a book and film to me. The former is *The Man in the High Castle* by Philip K. Dick and the latter, *Dark Blue World*, about a squadron of Czech pilots in World War II. He is so inspirationally patient and forbearing as he cannot move in bed, and watches movies overnight. A very brave man.

O reappears and begins chatting. He tells me about the three-year degree course that is now mandatory for a nursing qualification. He confirms that the number of British undergraduates has dropped dramatically since the introduction of student fees. As a mature student, he is able to fund himself. He is rather critical of the course, as he thinks it concentrates on technical skills and there is not enough on patient care. He says they spend three hours practising injections into a rubber arm or leg. During their hospital time, a trainee nurse works under a mentor. However, he thinks that students spend too much time listening and watching, and not doing. This means that he has never actually administered an injection into a frontal sinus cannula – i.e. the bolts in my head. You have to lift the caps off the top of the bolt and inject fluid directly into the frontal sinuses, which are above my eyes. Although it is an unusual procedure, it does not appear to be that difficult, but is normally done by a senior nurse.

As O's mentor is about to start the procedure, I ask if he would allow O to do it. I assure him that I would be responsible for any risk. It is agreed and O completes the task and steps back like a man who has just won the European Arm-Wrestling Championships.

This once again gets me thinking about the NHS and how nurses and doctors are trained. I wonder how much of the degree course is given over to interaction with patients. How much to talking to them, calming them down, and showing them love and compassion, when they are in pain, lonely and missing their loved ones? Surely this is as important as – if not more important than – putting in a cannula.

He explains that another problem is that, unlike other undergraduates, they cannot take part-time jobs to supplement their income as they have to work such long shifts, including many a night.

5.00pm   Go for a walk around the hospital.

Again, I am troubled by the lack of acknowledgment from the medical staff. Maybe it is my Frankenstein's Monster appearance, but nobody looks up, says anything or smiles, even if I say, "Hi." I get no recognition that I exist, even from the nurse who is looking after me for the day. The majority look at the floor and from those who do make eye contact there are only a few smiles.

10.00pm   Final IV of the day.

I try to sleep but can't and worry that I am hallucinating. I recall the words of T.S. Eliot in *Little Gidding* from *The Four Quartets*:

"We shall not cease from exploration
And the end of all our exploring
Will be to arrive where we started
And know the place for the first time."

Do we return to a point where we recognise who we really are or should have been, rather than who we actually became?

1 am. Unable to sleep so go for a walk feeling very depressed. No activity in the ward and a young nurse at the desk asks me if there's anything that I need. There isn't unless there is a remedy for feeling lost and lonely and a failure! Why had I made so many mistakes in life? I walk to the patient's sitting room which doubles up as a place where the physiotherapists help recovering disabled patients climb steps. There is in the corner a set of steps on which they practise.

The inspirational poem remains hidden behind the curtain.

I sit, and, after a few moments become transfixed by the steps. I start to cry uncontrollably. I can't take my eyes of the steps and my tears flow.

What the hell am I depressed about? I am alive, not disabled and with a problem that is hopefully treatable.

So why am I so depressed? There are so many others here so much worse off than I am and show remarkable levels of courage. Am I just wallowing in self pity?

I think of my so-called failures, but where they actually failures? Did they actually do me any harm? Did I suffer physically, mentally, socially or financially? No, I just didn't achieve what I presumptuously believed I should.

I was just too proud and arrogant.

As I sit sobbing I am suddenly visited, like Scrooge, by a ghost of things past, in the form of a memory of an incident, which I had long since forgotten. The memories return like videos.

This particular video reminds me of a catastrophic court appearance as a young solicitor.

One of my colleagues had gone on holiday, leaving me with a divorce case to be presented the following day. It was what was known as an "undefended divorce" as the respondent was not apparently contesting it. My colleague reassured me that it was a routine matter and gave me instructions as to how I should call the female petitioner to the witness stand and go through the facts in the petition with her, and then ask the judge for a divorce(a decree nisi)but for it to be expedited as the petitioner had arranged to remarry later in the week.

So I called a pleasant lady, and set about my task:

"Name"

"Date of marriage"

"Husband left on such and such a date" et cetera.

I turned to ask the judge for the decree, when he asked the woman whether her husband had ever attempted to come back.

"Yes" she replied "many times" but Bill (her husband to be) "had threatened him if he did not agree to the divorce."

The judge, a particularly pedantic and nasty individual who strongly disagreed with solicitors having rights of audience in his court, previously the exclusive domain of barristers, suggested to me with an almost orgasmic smugness and delight that the petition appeared to be flawed.

I stood, my mind, a total blank, when one of the barristers sitting alongside me(there were many in court that day waiting for their cases to be heard) whispered to me "seek to amend under order, 112".

"With respect Your Honour" I said, my mind re-engaging "could I respectfully seek to amend the petition under order 112"

He picked up a large, green book, which I had never seen before, opened it, and handed it to me via the clerk of the court, with a look of a man who just won the lottery.

"Perhaps you would be so kind as to read the order for the benefit of the court Mr Bennett" he said as if the lottery prize had just trebled.

"Order 112" I started, as I began to read the page "the service of proceedings in Papua New Guinea…"

"And the relevance, in this case Mr Bennett?" The

judge said, as if he was now spending the lottery prize money on a permanent supply of the finest vintage port.

I went into full-breakdown-manic -bullshit mode, like a man pleading for his life.

He interrupted me to pronounce judgement, and in my punch drunk state, I was sure I saw him put on the black cap, before passing the death sentence.

"Mr Bennett, you may think of yourself as something of a philosopher, but a lawyer you are certainly not" which could only just be heard above the tumultuous laughter that had engulfed the court.

He continued, barely suppressing a smile that I suspect had not been seen in judicial circles for many years, "The Petition is refused"

I thought that I could make my escape,without having any contact with the petitioner and her fiance but a voice rang out across the crowded waiting area

'Oi fuckin Ken Dodd"

I turned, and it was obviously Bill; very, very large, bald unshaven and without a full set of teeth. A man whose predisposition to violence was not buried in his Freudian subconscious, but was plain to see by a blind man in a darkened room, confirmed by a tattoo on his forehead reading "fuck off".

Before I had time to explain the mysteries and vagaries of the law, or the misfortune of appearing, before, a miserable, cantankerous judge more interested in my humiliation than justice, and the blossoming of a loving relationship Bill said, with a tone that indicated there was no room for negotiation"you owe me the fuckin 200 quid that I paid as a deposit for a wedding reception next Saturday at the working men's club, you useless bastard"

I was completely broke at the time, but realised immediately that my failure to pay would involve major physical rather than financial damage so I immediately agreed that he could pick up the cash from my office the following day.

On arriving back at the office, following the incident, my receptionist said "my God, you look like you've seen a ghost"

"I have" I said "the ghost of 200 quid lost"

Bill picked up the money, the following day, telling the receptionist and the clients in the waiting room that they should avoid me like the fuckin plague.

The following day, the local newspaper ran a headline; Undefended divorce thrown out by judge, criticising incompetent solicitor".

But Fortuna ,the Goddess of good luck generously came to my rescue and the the newspaper quoted the name of the solicitor on the petition, who was my colleague, rather than the "useless bastard" who had appeared. My reputation remained untarnished with the general public, but not with my colleague who required a years free drinks as compensation for damage to his own reputation. Fortunately, he was an extremely good solicitor and went on to have an outstanding and successful career.

I had a severe lecture from my bank manager who felt obliged in the circumstances to increase my overdraft yet again.

As this memory replayed in my mind, I found that I had stopped crying, and had started to laugh.

Of course, failures are almost always not setbacks but lessons by which we are taught, for example that making a mistake is the way by which we learn or that we are going in the wrong direction, or an ugly trait like arrogance is being tempered in the fire of humility or humiliation.

My court appearance was obviously a failure, but also an important lesson that I had learned many years before in the Boy Scouts:"Be Prepared".

I went back to bed and to sleep almost immediately.

"A hero is an ordinary individual who finds the strength to persevere and endure in spite of overwhelming obstacles."
Christopher Reeves

Dedicated to Brian

9

Waterloo Grammar School

Following my fortunate escape from having to attend the local public school, I started at WGS in 1956. By far the greatest benefit from the school was not educational, as I shall recount in due course, but the group of friends who remained friends to this day, six decades on: Bob Bagot ("Baig"); Ken Williams ("Ken"); both of whom have sadly died since I completed this book; Roger Morris ("Rog"); John Crompton ("Crom" and now "Prof Crompton" in the US); and the aforementioned "Crusty" Stephens. Ken, Rog and Crusty lived near me so we would walk to school and back every day (approximately 4½ miles), whereas Baig and Crom lived north of the school and got a train. Their positive influence shaped my life in profoundly meaningful ways, and I owe them all so much, together with the lifelong inspiration and love of my metal spoon-wielding brother, John.

The school was built in 1912 and was a solid, red brick building characteristic of the period. It was small. It only had about 450 pupils, but it had an interesting social, demographic mix. The school was close to the sea, and its selection area was large, stretching from Formby to the north to Litherland, where I lived, Seaforth and Bootle near the docks to the south. This produced pupils from different social classes, ranging from the middle-class children from the more affluent Formby to pupils from lower-middle and working-classes from the south.

Fortunately, all this made no difference to how well we integrated. The key difference lay between "The Sportsmen" and the rest, including the academics. The sportsmen were the stars. To represent the first team at football or cricket far exceeded in status any of those with outstanding academic ability. I was reasonably good at sports, particularly football, so my group of friends were self-selecting sportsmen.

The demographic selection produced an interesting division in sporting ability. Boys from the area south of the school (lower-middle and working-class) were better footballers than the northern group who were better cricketers and tennis-players. Grammar schools closer to the centre of Liverpool produced better football teams, whereas we were almost unbeatable at cricket. I remember one home match when we scored 168 and bowled out the opposition for two, one of these being a bye.

Unlike so many schools today, the facilities were basic, particularly the sporting ones. We had four football pitches – next to a refuse tip – all of which sloped dramatically.

During the summer, these pitches became the cricket ground. As we had two extremely fast bowlers – Baig and Crom – a score of two was no mean feat.

The school was no academic hothouse but had an eclectic group of masters who wore gowns. I suspect, looking back, some were suffering from post-traumatic stress disorder (PTSD), having served in the second world war. There were a couple of heavy drinkers and some who showed an unnatural level of violence. One master could hit you with a wooden board-duster from 30 feet without even turning around. He was much admired!

Caning was a regular occurrence – administered – to the hand or backside, depending on the preference of the day and the level of fitness, mentally and physically.

I loved the school and sailed blissfully on towards the sixth form.

I had always wanted to be a doctor but realised rather too late that it was not through any deep desire to heal the sick or develop ground-breaking medical innovations. There was a TV programme, *Dr Kildare*, with Richard Chamberlain. With his white coat and stethoscope, women adored him on sight. So, I thought, if I just got a white coat and stethoscope, I would become a female honeypot.

I took O levels and got decent marks in the arts subjects, but not so good in science, and just scraped a pass in French. I then made a catastrophic mistake of sticking with my Dr Kildare ambition and took A level physics, chemistry and biology, allowing my lustful fantasies of semi-naked nurses to overcome the fact that I had the scientific mind of a five-year-old. Careers advice did not seem to involve telling you the subjects that you should not, under any circumstances, take at A level.

I attended my careers interview. The careers master taught chemistry and made a variety of liquors for consumption both during and between lessons. We would occasionally be offered a "tasting" during which he would critique his latest vintage as "having a good nose," or being "a little heavy on the palate" and other phrases commonly used by connoisseurs of fine wines, notwithstanding the fact that you could run a car on his particular fermentation.

"So, Bennett," he slurred, offering me a small glass of his latest vintage, which he described as "young but fruity". "What have you in mind for the future?"

"A doctor, sir," I replied confidently.

"A doctor, a doctor," he replied with a look of horror, and requiring a top-up. "A doctor," he reminded himself. "But, why?"

Using my prepared lines, I said, "Because I have a calling to heal the sick, sir," my mind racing with the thought of nurses in a bra and pants.

After a couple more mouthfuls of that "young but fruity" intoxicant, and turning slightly pale, he said, "Nonsense, Bennett! Absolute nonsense! I know what you are made for."

"Indeed, sir."

"Without doubt, Bennett, the fire service!"

"A fireman?!" I replied.

"Most certainly, Bennett," he added, taking in some more of the soothing balm.

"But I have never thought about the fire service. My calling to work with the sick and the disabled is very strong, sir." (Control yourself, Bennett. She has taken off her underwear.)

"No, Bennett, absolutely absurd. You were born for the fire service. I have seen you in the chemistry lab, and your ability to endure heat is quite exceptional. Also, I think the helmet and uniform would suit you, and you are a big, strong boy so you could handle a hose easily. You sure you wouldn't like a drop of this restorative?"

"No thank you, sir, football match this afternoon."

"Of course, I quite forgot. Well, off you go, Bennett, and I look forward to seeing you in the local fire station in the future," he said with the look of a man who had converted a sinner and redirected him onto the path of righteousness.

That evening, I walked home facing a potentially life-changing decision. A life of high-speed motoring, great kit and heroic actions, saving people from burning houses and cats from tall trees? A man, respected and admired, doing worthy work for the benefit of society or the potential seduction of a bevy of large-breasted nurses? I was confused. *What do I know about being a doctor other than what I see on TV?* I thought as I meandered along. Suddenly, my musings were interrupted by a shiny red fire engine, speeding past with bells ringing and warriors clad in majestic fireproof armour. I wavered for a second before I suddenly remembered a key factor in my decision – I suffered from car sickness! So, the nurses triumphed! I have felt the occasional pang of conscience and guilt as to the number of cats who may have suffered a tragic end, stuck in the unforgiving foliage of a mighty oak tree because of my decision.

I embarked instead on my scientific odyssey, to study physics, chemistry and biology, but, alas, my dreams of steamy, passionate nights in the nurses' hostel proved elusive because I was, to put it bluntly, absolutely hopeless at my chosen subjects.

Physics

I quickly realised that I had joined a science cult of boys whose ambitions ranged from converting urine into water to solving the world's fuel shortage to building a car fuelled by cornflakes, or to discover whether penguins could fly backwards. It was as if I had moved to a foreign country whose language I could not speak.

I even exchanged my subscription from *Football Monthly* to the *New Scientist*, but, alas, I couldn't understand a word of it. My colleagues were always banging on about Galileo, who I had taken to be a Brazilian footballer, or whether Einstein's theory of relativity confirmed the existence of black holes. What Einstein had to do with the mining industry I have never understood!

So, having in fact failed to understand almost everything, I resorted to my one remaining hope: cheating. A significant part of the exam was a practical exercise, where we had to perform an experiment and produce empirical data and graphs. We could file in and take any place available in the lab. There was a boy in my class who later became professor of physics at a redbrick university. So, my plan was simple: sit next to him and repeat everything he did, record the data and draw the graphs, as he was bound to be right (as indeed he was).

I left the lab like someone who had just won *Mastermind*. I was a physicist!

Alas, the examiner had anticipated my cunning plan, and the person sitting next to me was answering a different question!

Chemistry

This involved standing around bottles of acid and other dangerous substances, trying to decide what a particular substance was, e.g. sodium chloride, potassium nitrate etc. Again, I plumbed the depths of academic ineptitude. However, I did receive recognition of an unusual kind. Several years before, a boy had blown himself up along with a section of the chemistry lab. He was dispatched to hospital and never seen again, although I heard he had made an excellent recovery and gone on to study Minoan Erotic Art at university. However, the shredded remains of his green laboratory coat (which we had to wear during the lessons) had survived. It was known as the "JL Memorial Coat". The master decided that whoever was at the bottom of the class would wear the remaining part of the coat to humiliate the pupil into trying harder and improving, and so pass the coat on to another slacker to be mocked. I wore the garment with pride throughout my entire sixth form career. Nobody else got close!

The other good news was that we were all going to pass, because the chemistry master generously provided the answers to all the questions. To my dismay, he was caught as I was entering the upper sixth. Sadly, his replacement was not so accommodating, and yet again I faced the traumatic experience of failure. I did, however, ask if I could keep the "JL Memorial Coat" but was told by the chemistry master, "No Bennett. There will always be another clown like you."

Biology

Biology proved a change of environment. My school did not do A level biology, so my friend Crusty and I become new boys in the neighbouring girls' high school. Paradise, we thought. We bought a tandem to provide a grand arrival outside the girls' sixth form room. Alas, as we swung around the school, waving to our new fans in the sixth form room, we hit a pothole and were unseated. Crusty tore a trouser leg, and I damaged part of the sleeve of my jacket. The girls' laughter, continued for as long as it took to make us presentable before meeting the headmistress, Miss Jagger, and our new classmates.

Miss Jagger looked like a member of the SS who hadn't been informed that the war had ended 20 years earlier. Her opening line was, "I totally deplore the mixing of sexes in co-education," delivered in what I thought was a slight German accent. "The slightest sign of impropriety will be severely punished," she continued, picking up a long, hefty ruler that lay on her desk. "You will be constantly chaperoned by a teacher, and do not, under any circumstances, talk to any of the girls."

Her final look indicated that any punishment would indeed be severe, as she waved the ruler at us. I noticed that one side was razor-sharp, and on the other, I thought I detected what appeared to be congealed blood.

On our way to meet our female fellow students, I asked for permission to go to the toilet. This threw our chaperone, Miss Stott, who was to teach us biology, into a complete panic. They had not considered the latrine facilities. Anyway, after a few moments of intense consideration, she took me to the girls' toilets. She asked me firmly to stand back and shouted, "All girls out! Boy coming!" This was evidently the *cri de coeur* if ever a boy visited the school. Out poured a gaggle of giggling girls pointing at me and laughing hysterically. I entered the chamber and the thought suddenly occurred to me: I had never been in a girls' toilet before, and I was struck immediately by the fact that there were no urinals stuck to the walls to test your power and accuracy. There were only cubicles. I cautiously opened a door, afraid that female ablutions may somehow involve equipment new to a male user. But no, they were the same as ours, except they were much smaller, and the seat was much closer to the floor. I was in the junior section! Weighing 13 stone 7 pounds, I lowered myself carefully onto the seat, thinking it would not be a good start to demolish the bowl. I relaxed and set about preparing for my stress evacuation. I looked up at the door, and to my horror there was a sign which read, "DON'T PANIC!" *About what?* I thought and began to panic.

Our teacher was a spinster, aged about 45 and dressed like the stereotype of a spinster – hair in a bun with heavy brogue shoes and a woollen dress, three sizes too large so as to disguise her feminine form. We quickly discovered that she loved "her boys" and would at any opportunity get as close as possible without risking legal proceedings. Leaning over me to examine my dissection of a frog became an erotic experience.

Crusty and I soon learned that these strange creatures, although outwardly very intelligent, charming, gentle and funny were as competitive as Wonder Woman. The truth was starkly revealed when he and I decided to challenge the girls to a game of hockey. Our school did not play hockey, so we thought that it would be a good bonding opportunity for those boys who had limited contact with girls, which was all of us. We raised a team (applications heavily oversubscribed), borrowed some kit and arrived for a 3pm "bully-off" at the girls' school.

In my pre-match team talk, I emphasised that "bully-off" was a technical term and not a call to arms. "These are girls," I said, "and must be treated with gentlemanly courtesy and with respect for their inferior physicality. So, just think of it as a social event."

I warned them that the girls would be wearing sports attire and, tempting as it might be, any inappropriate behaviour would result in an immediate sending-off. It was, I think, a speech that would have been approved by the #metoo movement.

Within minutes of "bullying off", we grasped that the girls had not in fact seen this as a bonding activity. They were vicious, cunning, brutal and uncompromising. They had a defender who could best be described as "big-boned", a girl who could take a small African country at the weekend, armed only with a hockey stick. By half-time, she had reduced our side of 11 to just nine, with a third admitted to hospital in the second half. We didn't even have the pleasure of enjoying a communal shower.

Academically, biology proved yet another fiasco. One part of the exam was to dissect a rat. We practiced religiously at school in the lab. It was apparent in my first attempt that surgery was not my strong point. The wretched creature would be pulled out of a tank of formaldehyde placed in front of us, and we had, for example, to expose liver, kidney or some other part, with limited bloodshed. At least one girl was destined for a career in neurosurgery. I, in contrast, was Vlad the Impaler. My rat was never on the board, but in pieces scattered around the lab with me and the lab covered in blood.

One day it occurred to me that my rat had not expired but had in fact taken one look at me, screamed, "Oh fuck! Not him!" and committed suicide.

"Education is an admirable thing, but it is well to remember from time to time that nothing that is worth knowing can be taught."
Oscar Wilde

10

Friendship

I have been extremely lucky in life to have a number of true friends. Not many, certainly fewer than 10. Some, who I have already mentioned, I met at school, and some during my later life who I will not embarrass by naming, but who know who they are. Their guidance, inspiration and constant support throughout my many medical problems have not only shaped my life but have kept me from straying too far into Dante's "Dark Wood". Friends help us to overcome our lack of self-discipline.

I resolved to write a brief profile of each of them to highlight their uniqueness and to recognise their special contribution to my life and place in my heart. But I have failed! I don't know whether this is down to a lack of literary talent, but my attempts seem to create caricatures that do not do them justice and fail to express my appreciation and love for them. So I have chosen, instead, to write in general terms about what I believe it is that creates these rare and particular relationships which have been so life-enhancing. The views I express are not my own but are based on the writings of two great classical philosophers and men of letters, Aristotle and Cicero, whose essays on the subject I would recommend to you.

1. Friendship is only possible between "good men".
2. It is so inimitable that its embodiment must be restricted to a small number of people. We can have many acquaintances who we like and admire, but we can only have a few real friends.
3. Friendship is a complete feeling about someone, strengthened by mutual good will and affection. It can be regarded as the greatest gift we have been given, but without goodness it cannot exist.
4. The benefits of friendship almost defy description they are so great. Is this why I couldn't write about my own friends? Can life be worth living without friends? Is there a more satisfying experience in the world than to have someone with whom you can talk about any and all subjects? If life is tough, can trials be borne without someone who you know and who cares about you unconditionally?
5. Friendship provides hope for the future. It maintains our optimism that assistance will always be at hand and, even in death, the inspiration, love and comfort live on in our hearts as I have found with Baig and Ken.

6. Someone once said that "No man is an island," but I gave it a shot, before recognizing the emptiness of that life.

7. Friendship is built on love, independent of any calculation of profit. Sometimes people may pretend to be your friend, to gain some benefit, particularly if you are successful. But real friendship involves no element of falsity or pretence. Friendship is sincere and genuine; it comes from a feeling of affection and inclination of the heart.

8. Friendship causes us to seek out and enjoy the company and character of the friend, to reciprocate their friendship, and to desire to perform services on their behalf without demanding any for oneself in return. A friend is always ready to help and never hangs back.

9. Always listen to your friend's advice, however severe. True friendship develops our most important quality: self-awareness. We see ourselves most clearly through the eyes of those who love us.

10. The foundation of friendship is trust. Trust and friendship go together. Also, a true friend will not enjoy criticising you, and when others criticise you will not listen, and will not believe or entertain that you have done wrong.

11. True friendship seems natural, relaxed and easy. It is truly pleasurable and timeless.

12. You may not see your friend for a year and then

when you do it is as you had last met them the day before. Conversation flows immediately and spontaneously, and time stops. It is like the opposite poles of a magnet attracting.

All of the above applies to – and serves as an inadequate thank-you to – the small band of my special friends who have tolerated my failings and eccentricities and stuck with me over so many years. At the end of the day, I must agree with the words of W.H. Auden: "Among those whom I like or admire I can find no common denominator, but among those I love, I can; all of them make me laugh."

And for those who have never met me and never will, I would ask you to remember the words of Martin Luther King: "Hate cannot drive out hate, only love can do that."

"We should be careful
Of each other, we should be kind
While there is time."
Philip Larkin, "The Mower"

11

Return to Reality
(and After School)

My memories had caused me to feel trapped once again, controlled, helpless and very tired. Why? Firstly, I have become irritated by the fact that on the ward door I am Peter Bennet 28C. It may seem trivial, but in my present state, the loss of a T takes on a disproportionate emotional gravity. I suggest a couple of times, in a courteous and jovial matter, that I am Bennett with two Ts. I tried to add a T myself, but self-editing requires a special pen. I tell another nurse what a shock it is to lose a T. I have always been rather proud of being a two-T Bennett and feel somehow diminished and depressed. I told the rather nice Romanian nurse that the only upside to being the new Mr Bennet was that I could be in *Pride and Prejudice* without changing my name, but from the blank look on her face I don't think that the book is widely read in Romania. A few hours later I notice that a T has been added with a secret pen. I now feel more like my old self.

Secondly, I begin to realise how easy it is to become institutionalized. You are no longer a person with a name, history, emotions, fears, in a stressful and painful situation. Patients, often elderly and confused, are separated from their loved ones. The staff are in control. I recall the famous experiment conducted in Stanford University in the US. A group of students were randomly divided into two groups. For 14 days one group were to be guards and the other prisoners in a mocked-up prison. The experiment had to be abandoned early because the guards had started to exhibit aggressive, controlling characteristics, and the prisoners had become passive and submissive.

Further studies have shown how easy and quickly our personalities can shift towards the dominant and cruel if unrestrained. It's a subconscious process where a group's behaviour can change, even within a hospital. Recent examples of cover-ups in hospitals in Staffordshire and Tyneside have revealed the potentially catastrophic results of staff becoming arrogant, negligent and uncaring.

Fareed Zakaria, in his must-read book, *Ten Lessons for a Post-Pandemic World*, referred to in my introduction, examines the conflict that has developed as part of a "populist" philosophy between so-called "experts" in various fields and large sections of society who doubt and indeed deny the evidence that experts produce.

This has been seen with the potentially disastrous

consequences in the Covid pandemic, subsequent miraculous vaccine discovery, and vaccination-implementation. People with absolutely no knowledge of the subject will fail to accept the advice of medical experts who have spent their lives studying viruses and creating vaccines to defeat and indeed eradicate them. Smallpox, for example, had been endemic in populous areas, largely China and India in the 6th century and America in the 16th. Smallpox vaccination was known as variolation before the modern practice of vaccination with cowpox (vaccinia) was demonstrated in 1796. In 1959 the USSR suggested a campaign that depended on production of heat-stable vaccines and a reusable, prolonged needle that used little material. In that year alone, 59 countries experienced cases. When the intensified eradication programme began in 1967 there were 35 countries with a total population of 1.2 billion. Over 10 million contracted the disease and two million died. The world eradication took 10 years at a cost of $83 million for foreign assistance and about $160 million spent by individual countries. Compare this with the estimated $2 billion spent annually to control smallpox. The last known case was in October 1977. In 1980 the 33rd World Health Assembly (WHO) declared that smallpox had been eradicated.[1]

We know international investment in antibacterial/ viral vaccines has been reduced in the last 10 years. Let the smallpox example remind us of the need for well-funded international cooperation to detect and quickly eradicate

---

1   Information from the National Library of Medicine in the USA

pathogens. Those who have developed the anti-Covid vaccines deserve our eternal praise and credit.

As Michael Gove said famously during the Brexit debate, "I think the people of this country have had enough of experts." Fine words from an Oxbridge intellectual who feels entitled to tell us how to run the country and our own lives.

We need the best trained experts in many aspects of life, for example, medicine, engineering, computer science and education, who understand their speciality to a high degree, but also, and perhaps more importantly, we urgently need leaders who understand and care about us and our futures by acting and not just talking.

What should be done to protect patients from abuse? Whistle-blowers' complaints should – initially, and anonymously – be investigated by a panel made up of a doctor, a lawyer and a layperson, all independent of the hospital. If the complaint is found to be a valid one that requires, for example, some operational change, the panel should report its recommendations to the trust's chief executive and to the head of the department involved with the time required for the changes to be introduced and the panel satisfied. If it isn't, then penalties should apply. NHS workers are advised to raise concerns with line managers and there is the Care Quality Commission. They are in fact told that it is their duty to report any concerns about unsafe work practices or lack of care by other professionals, but being a whistle-blower is still frowned upon in many places and there are few safeguards if they suffer an adverse reaction for revealing wrongdoing.

If the complaint is serious, the matter must be referred to the police. If proved, the consequences should be severe – e.g. dismissal, with no pay-off or pension enhancement. The whole process should be *independent* of the hospital and its staff.

There should be regular training recognising the danger and reminding all those concerned of the Stanford experiment, and the very high duty of care expected from those who treat us. We are individual humans as well as patients. Nobody on the ward knew Brian had been married for 62 years and had a son in America who was a consultant radiologist.

I try to relax and sleep but am stressed and tired and haunted by the words spoken at the end of Ken Loach's brilliant film *I, Daniel Blake*. At Blake's funeral, Katie who had two children and who he had befriended and helped, says, "They call it the pauper's funeral because it is the cheapest slot at 9am. But Dan was not a pauper to us. He gave us things money can't buy. When he died, I found this on him. He always used to write in pencil [he was a skilled carpenter who had to stop work because of an accident]. And he wanted to read it at his appeal, but he never got the chance to. And I swear that that this lovely man had so much more to give, and that the state drove him to an early grave. And this is what he wrote: 'I am not a client, a customer, nor a service-user. I am not a shirker, a scrounger, a beggar, nor a thief. I'm not a National Insurance number or blip on a screen. I paid my dues, never a penny short, and proud to do so. I don't tug the forelock but look my neighbour in the eye and help him if I can. I don't accept or seek charity. My name is Daniel Blake. I am a man, not a dog. As such, I demand my rights. I demand you treat me with respect. I, Daniel Blake, am a citizen, nothing more and nothing less. Thank you.'"

I try to sleep, tears rolling down my cheeks, and think of Oskar Schindler's words at the end of the film Schindler's List: "I could have done more."

Should I have done more? Of course, I should. Ultimately, whatever our backgrounds, culture, religion or point of view, to survive we have to look after each other. Or we will reach the point expressed by Woody Allen, "more than any other time in history, mankind faces a crossroads. One path leads to despair and utter hopelessness, the other to total extinction. Let us hope that we have the wisdom to choose correctly."

6.00pm   Headline in *The Times*: "Spend extra cash on more doctors and nurses, urge voters." But will it be done?

As Henry Marsh writes with passion in his book *Do No Harm*, having to train junior doctors and the risk involved in them undertaking surgery that is typically performed by registrars and consultants makes him consider: "Why don't I just stop training junior doctors? Why should I have to carry the burden of deciding whether they can operate or not when fucking management and politicians decide their training. The country's massively in debt financially, why not have a massive debt of medical expertise as well?

Fuck the management, fuck the government and fuck the politicians and their fiddled expenses and fuck all the civil servants in the Department of Health."

The days are long and stressful, and with sleep-deprivation I find my mind is regularly reflecting on my earlier life. I have done well in life, but I did not have a promising start.

After my abysmal exam performance, I set off with my friends to hitchhike to Denmark and have some fun. My mother sent me the results. The lord moves in mysterious ways. Three passes at the lowest grades. So, I wrote to her and told her to throw out the stethoscope and white coat I kept in my bedroom. I fell in love with Elsa, a Danish pastry, and cancelled my subscription to *The Naturalist*. No more photos for me. I had in fact become rather bored by the predictability of the magazine, which consisted mainly of nude couples playing volleyball, particularly as the standard of the British squad was lamentably poor. My final copy showed a couple of Brits, represented by a clinically obese man whose willy was lost in a thicket of neatly arranged pubic hair. His partner's breasts conclusively proved Newton's theory of gravity, as she could not stand upright. On the opposite side of the net were a couple of blond Scandinavians. His inner thigh was bruised due to being struck regularly by an unusually large schlong, like a clapper striking a church bell. She was a Scandinavian goddess, and I wondered whether, during the game, our man's pecker might attempt to escape the shrubbery and see what it was missing. I have to admit that I did cut out the photo of the Nordic goddess for use as a future bookmark during my reading of *War and Peace*.

My mother, who lovingly believed in me unconditionally, kept writing to me pleading to decide what to do. One night, after a drinking competition against a team of Swedes, I asked one of them to open the *University Handbook* and pick a course for me.

"Swahili at the London School of African and Oriental Studies," he announced before passing out.

Remembering my language disorder, I asked the only Swede still conscious to have a go.

"Law," he slurred.

Law, I thought, sounded good even if I had never thought about it. It had a professional ring to it, like Medicine, unlike Geology or Computer Science. I, therefore, asked my mother to proceed with the application. Although she had left school at 14, she produced one of the great works of fiction. I was a boy passionate about justice, grade 5 on the clarinet, an accomplished ballroom dancer, outstanding all-round sportsman and undertook a range of charitable activities. The application was a masterpiece and secured me an interview in Birmingham. I had a tearful parting from my beautiful Scandinavian inamorata. We pledged our eternal love which, like most teenage holiday romances, became an enjoyable memory, after the exchange of a number of passionate letters. No internet photos then, thank God!

The chap who interviewed me at Aston showed no interest in me as a genuinely Renaissance man but only that I had played football at regional level at school. He was particularly keen on soccer. No probing intellectual questions but a simple statement after five minutes: "Good, well, I look forward to seeing you at the trials in October.

I commenced my three-year degree in Law in October, and played in the trial, got in the first team, damaged my ankle and never played again.

Who was it who said, "The law is an ass,"? We were encouraged to take the advice of Sir Edward Coke (1552-1634): "Six hours in sleep, in law's grave study six, six hours in prayer, the rest on Nature fix." Alas, it proved uninspiring, so I regressed into 10 hours' in sleep, in beer's grave study six, the rest on talking. I was saved from Dante's "Dark Wood" by two pieces of good fortune, one which would change my life.

I discovered that law suited the only part of my brain that operated reasonably well, my memory. I had one of those minds that remembered things precisely, but only for a short period, e.g. the facts that allow you to remember legal acts and cases and repeat them in an exam paper. It certainly wasn't a method that would propel me to the highest levels of the legal profession because within days it would all be forgotten. However, it got me a pass with no lasting memory of law whatsoever.

The only subject I enjoyed was Roman law because of the young female lecturer in the first year. She had the longest, most beautiful legs I had ever seen, which she would wrap around each other like a vine on a tree while wearing a fashionable miniskirt. At the end of each lecture I would require several minutes of repose before standing up to avoid a potentially life-changing injury or expensive tailor's bills.

But, in the darkness, a star appeared that would lighten my life for the next 55 years. I met my wife, Sarah, who arrived a year after me. On the 4th of December, 2021, we celebrated our 50th wedding anniversary staying at the same hotel where we had spent our first. 50 years adds up to 18, 263 days, which gave me time to write a poem about her. We came from different backgrounds, she from a small estate in Northamptonshire and me from a lower middle-class semi in Liverpool. The power and mystery of love. But more of love later. On our anniversary I wrote

"THE GIRL FROM THE COVER OF COUNTRY LIFE"

There was a young girl from Whilton, who led all the local boys on,
But in 1971, some say to be "cool", she married a boy from the Pool.
Her parents had hoped, as all parents do, that she'd marry a man of repute,
With a house, some land, and maybe a "shoot".
But to their horror, instead, she decided to wed,
A penniless young Scouser, who was keen to espouse her,
Who spoke with an accent exceedingly rare, lived in a flat exceedingly bare,
And if you wanted a laugh, had one to spare.
But many there were who looked on, sighed, "Oh, she must be a fool,"

For they never stay married, those boys from the Pool.
But, with love in their hearts, they were never to part,
For she thought, funny was better than money!

They met, so legend tells, not with the sound of Bow bells,
But in a city called Brum, to whither they'd come,
To pursue the study of Law (he a year before): and maybe
more,
To dream, and sing and fall in love, with Eros watching
from above.
Drinking too much beer, lectures missed, or blunders
kissed,
And waking tired and pale, would learn without fail,
The danger of too much ale.

I (for the young man was me), spent my first year
unattached and free,
The study of Law proved rather boring for me.
Although it had its moments, when studying the Romans.
I pondered a divorce from the Law, on the grounds of her
unreasonable behaviour,
And no sign of beauty to be my saviour!
So, wearing the mask of a clown, my sorrows I did drown,
in the Stygian gloom of Newcastle Brown.

But on one dull October day, began the end of my dismay,
For on that day my life was changed, my heart and mind
both rearranged,
For in the bar an Angel appeared, a drunken vision, so I
feared,

A vision so beautiful and fair, that I put down my pint to
sit and stare.
Her hair was dark, her eyes so brown, her skin so soft and
lips so rare,
My heart was beating, oh so fast, I thought each breath
would be my last.
She wore a grey fitted coat, pearls and cashmere jumper,
that made my heart go thumper and thumper!!

A drunken illusion must have caused this strife, for
before me stood
The Girl from the cover of *Country Life*.
She was escorted by a man who wore a jacket, brogues
and tie, so I knew it was pointless to try!

My God, I said to my friends assembled, have you seen
anything that could resemble,
A girl with such wondrous charms, she's the Venus de
Milo with arms!!
"Too good for the likes of you," they laughed, "but we'll
bet you a pound
She'll make no sound."

Emboldened with leonine courage, and with friends to
encourage,
I walked with James Bond's self-confident air, determined
a name to obtain from her.
But as those brown eyes stared, I became so scared,
That I only mumbled, and like the Cowardly Lion just
crumbled,

My only hope from the depth of my blues,
Was I noticed she was wearing bright green shoes!!

That night did Eros visit me, and tell me of my fate, that
the Cowardly Lion had met his mate,
And would spend the rest of his life,
With the Girl from *Country Life*.

So next morning I awoke, like Dante from the darkest
wood,
To search without cease for My Beatrice.
And with Fortuna by my side, to the library I sped
Where I was told a studious life she led.
"Are you a student?" the Librarian whispered, as only
librarians can.
"2nd year," I replied, slightly tongue-tied,
As she stroked her lower lip, with a large paperclip.
"But you've never been here before," she said coming
near, putting her lips so close to my ear.
"So, what do you want?" she purred, leaning so close as if
to kiss.
She was instantly both my Scylla and Charybdis.
"To find my true love," I sighed, "Who has been sent
from above,
By Eros and Aphrodite, to fill my heart with love."
"You're mad," she muttered meekly,
"But if your search is in vain, although I may be rather plain,
I am happy to be your Cupid twice weekly."
(But love is not love, which alters when opportunity finds
a pretty librarian so willing and kind.)

To my joy I found my inamorata, in Equity, Trusts and
the Law of Barter.

Our eyes met, well, I say *met*, for between hers and mine
stood her glasses.

(Who said, "A man should never make passes at girls who
wear glasses,"?)

But, neglecting this admonition, I noticed the specs'
position.

For the horizontal they did not seek, but an angle from
left eye to right cheek.

And I thought, *How sweet, the Girl from the* Country Life
cover,
Has one ear higher than the other.

"Have you seen *Dr. Zhivago*?" I stuttered. "No, I go to Dr
Clements," she muttered.

"No, the film," I stammered. "No," she mannered.

"Are you a foreign student?" she asked, "your English is
very good."

And I thought that in her sylvan idyll, where cows gently
chewed the cud,

Scouse was as clear as mud.

So *Zhivago* we saw,

"And our homeward step was just as light as the tap-
dancing feet of Astaire,"[2]

And we kissed and she smiled at me, tho' the night was
cold and misty,

---

2   Words from "A Nightingale Sang in Berkeley Square", lyrics by
Eric Maschwitz,

I knew that forever we would be Omar Sharif and Julie
Christie.
I have failed to deliver gifts that make a girl quiver and purr,
Handbags, jewels and expensive fake fur.
But for you, who deserves so much more, only words can
I offer,
No Orphean elegance do I possess, or clever lines that
might impress,
But in my simple, sentimental way, I merely want to say:
At night, when I sit by the fire, I'm so glad that I
disdained Fate's Liar,
And made passes at a girl who wore glasses.
For everlasting love began, which although we sometimes
try,
Will never ever die.

Tomorrow may be cloudy and colder, and you are
certainly older, and like a drop of whisky,
But you're still my Julie Christie,
For I know for me there is no life
Without that beautiful Girl from the cover of *Country Life*.

"The happiest marriages are low-level conflicts,
with territorial incursions, strafing and
devastating cold wars."
Author unknown

12

The People I Met
(and the *Why* Question)

Day Six – Tuesday 6th November, 2019

6.00am   IV

7.00am   The man in the bed opposite wakes, still
          moaning, and says he is going home today.
          Thank God.

Although he is going home, he is still unhappy. He is given
a cup of tea. Calls the nurse: "You can take this back. I
want weak tea with lots of milk."

Ten minutes later: "The cornflakes are too dry, not
enough milk."

The charming Polish grandmother (I still can't believe
it) appears. "Toast?" she asks.

"Brown wholemeal," he replies grumpily. "Don't be too long."

A new nurse comes to speak to him.

"Toast" he asks.

"Sorry," she replies.

"Toast with tea?" he says.

"Milk and sugar?" she asks.

"Lots of milk, no sugar," he replies grumpily.

"Some 15 minutes later, a cup of tea arrives with sugar, about which he complains to us for about 20 minutes.

10.00am   The world's laziest cleaner arrives and does his nine-second clean up and down the ward with his eyes seemingly closed, and leaning heavily on the brush. I am leaving traps all over the ward, e.g. bits of paper or tissues to test him. He fails every time.

The man in the bed opposite again: "Any more toast?"

Nurse: "I shall see."

"Brown wholemeal with plenty of butter and marmalade. I am starving."

I wonder whether he is a mystery patient, sent in to test the system to breaking point.

11.00am   Get a copy of the paper. A report claims Sheikh Mansour has funded Manchester City's transformation with billions of pounds.

His name is Mansour bin Zayid Sultan bin Khalifa Al

Nahyan. He's deputy prime minister of the United Arab Emirates, a member of the Abu Dhabi royal family, worth $49 billion. I muse on how he accumulated so much money. How did he start? Did he have a small market stall? Appear on *The Apprentice* or *Dragons' Den*? What does he do with it all? When other people have to live on $10 a day, why waste your money on a bunch of overpaid men who, by good fortune, can kick a ball straight? A footballer can earn more in a week than a doctor could save in a lifetime.

I recently read *Moneyland: Why Thieves and Crooks Now Rule the World and How to Take It Back*. By Oliver Bullough, a book about how corrupt leaders and immoral individuals cheat the system. Bullough writes, "We are witnessing the greatest shift of wealth from the poor to the rich in history. In the US alone, the wealthiest avoid paying an astonishing $53 billion in taxes each year, and the global total is now around $7 trillion." If a tenth of that was paid in tax, think of the difference it would make in overcoming global problems like poverty, slavery, the sex trade. How many innocent people would no longer starve or be exploited? How would the world's economy grow, particularly in Africa? And how much better would the NHS be?

It is utterly EVIL, and I am saddened to say that the city of London is one of the major players. I am angry and distressed to read this. What can we do? The government has promised to halt it, but little effort seems to be expended on what, together with climate change, poses the greatest threats to our planet.

It takes me about an hour to calm down, and I return to the paper and so move from the most critical decisions to the most trivial. "Tennis authorities debate whether players should get their own towels to dry themselves off after each point and not rely on a teenager to give them one which they then throw back."

It is a no-brainer. Of course they should handle their own towel, drenched in their own sweat. Why should a poor kid have to catch a towel covered in perspiration, slobber and mucus, and be at risk of catching an infection or skin disorder? Then, on top of that, receive a bollocking from a multi-millionaire if they drop it or have to reach for it.

Also, the player should be responsible for building their own towel rail from an IKEA kit. Do squash players have a break after an exhausting rally and towel themselves down? In the 1930s didn't Fred Perry or Bunny Austin just bring a clean towel which their mum had washed the night before, to mop their brow? Of course they didn't just sit down every two games. They stopped, had a quick ciggy and got on with it.

I remember once playing squash with someone who smoked during the match to calm his nerves, and another who played in ballet pumps as he was frightened of slipping! And an elderly player in Leicestershire who kept his jacket on throughout so as not to catch a chill. Sadly, I lost all three matches.

I'm on the internet to see if I can buy some kind of weapon to silence the man opposite who, when asked by the nurse if he is in pain, says, "All over."

"Would you like some paracetamol?" she asks.

"No, some more toast and a cup of tea [repeated three times] and no sugar."

My Slovak friend in the next bed tells me he was an outstanding ice-hockey player in his youth, which I can believe, as he is built like a bull. He has been lying in bed in the same position for three days. He asked for a wheelchair so he can sit up, but there appears to be a problem. He remains calm and patient. He is the complete opposite of the complainer on the other side. I get him drinks and provide chocolate biscuits.

Go the bathroom. Someone has used the towels, and instead of putting them in the domestic waste bin, two feet away, has left them on the floor and in the washbasin. Suspect it's the moaner opposite. Will interview him under caution later and, if no confession results, will call the KGB operative in the corridor to beat it out of him.

He gets another breakfast but does not say thank you, only, "The marmalade portions are too small."

Toilet. A truly momentous occasion. After six days we have a clean bathroom with blue disinfectant and a decent shower.

Man opposite: "Will the NHS provide a taxi to get me home?"

"No."

"Why not? They brought me here. I shall write to my MP."

Another of his phone calls ends with, "I give up."

The nurse arrives with medication and asks if he can see out of the other eye. (He has a patch on one eye).

"Yes," he replies, "but what happens when I get on and off a bus. I have to take three a day."

"Be careful," the nurse replies without a hint of irony.

She puts drops in his eye and leaves him. A minute later, having moved nothing but his mouth for 24 hours, he is out of the bed, running down the corridor like Usain Bolt, shouting, "It's stinging. It's stinging."

The nurse brings him back, reassuring him that everyone has some irritation after the drops. She asks whether he wants some lunch.

"No," he replies, "too much pain." (*Or was it the three breakfasts?* I think.)

11.00am   Cleaner appears and stops next to my bed. "Hi," I say, "how are you?" No reply. He moves the brush near the underside of the bed. *Wow,* I think, *a breakthrough!* But the brush is having none of it and pulls back. More handling and discipline-training required for the brush. These modern brushes!

11.30am   The plastic surgeons visit my Slovak friend next to me. They are, as usual, quick and to the point, and leave before he can gather his thoughts and ask a question.

He is on the phone to somebody; I suspect it is a girlfriend in Thailand. He is trying to explain why he can't arrive for a holiday. It sounds as if they don't know each other very well. Later, he tells me he would like to live in Thailand. I advise him to go.

I am now permanently on OWL Wi-Fi. The guy from *Countryside Watch* is telling me about different kinds of tits. In my present state, it is all too much!

12.00pm   Changed into a gown as worried my pyjamas were becoming a health hazard. The gown was definitely not designed by Vivienne Westwood. It is put on back to front with the back open, held together by three loose ties which regularly come undone, revealing my fragile wreck of a body. Ideal for Kim Kardashian.

The day drifts endlessly on. I am so tired. I find reading difficult and would confess to every atrocity committed since the Second World War. However, someone has brought me some easy reading: golf magazines. Although a golfer, I have never been keen on golf magazines. They contain tips and photographs from a 28-year-old, 6' 3" professional who practices eight hours a day and has been playing since he was four. What possible use that is to an overweight 74-year-old with poor eyesight and a back condition that restricts my backswing and follow-through to knee-height.

The golf magazines cause me to remember a lecture I gave at one of our local psychiatric hospitals, on patient safety and the law of negligence, which a bright young solicitor had written for me. The hospital was a magnificent 18th century building originally designed for affluent aristocratic families to deposit a member who was considered a lunatic. It had many famous patients including John Clare, the great English poet who was committed there in 1841. On arrival at the hospital, the accompanying doctor, one Fenwick Grimshire, was asked on the admission form, "was the insanity preceded by any severe or long-continued mental emotion?"

Dr Grimshire entered, "After poetical prosing."

No more Pam Ayres for me. Too risky!

I had a decent turnout of doctors, nurses and senior management and sat on the window ledge of a more modern building overlooking the hospital's own private nine-hole golf course. I reached the point in my lecture where I was discussing the hospital's potential negligence if patients harmed each other. As I glanced out of the window, I caught sight of a smartly dressed golfer throwing his clubs individually down the first fairway. He'd got to the short irons, so I turned to the audience and pointed out the potential legal consequences of another patient being struck by a club.

"Oh, that's James," said one of the doctors. "Harmless. Wouldn't hurt a fly."

"But, what if one of the clubs hits somebody," I enquired.

"He never does," replied the doctor. "Because a) he is an extremely accurate thrower, and b) he would never do it if anyone was in striking distance."

Fascinated by the incident, I asked whether there were any other eccentric golfers in the hospital.

"Well, there's Ted," a nurse announced, "who plays without a ball."

As a golfer, that struck me as unusual, so I enquired about how he played.

"He's awfully keen," she said without any hint that it may not be within PGA rules. "He's got all the best clubs, bag, shoes etc."

"But how does he play?" I asked.

"Well," she said, "he puts the tee in the ground, minus the ball, has a few practice swings, and then lets rip."

"And then?"

"Well, it depends on whether he has hit a good shot or a bad one. If it's a good one on the fairway, he plays his next shot. However, if it is a bad shot, he goes in the rough to look for it. If he doesn't find it, he has to go back to the tee to play another one. But, if he finds it, he has to decide whether he can reach the green or has to play out sideways onto the fairway. Sometimes he will stand next to a tree and curse his bad luck that he has no shot, and he has to take a drop. On the green, he lines up his non-existent ball and if he holes it, says, 'Well done, Ted!' and moves on to the second tee."

"He does it all the way around?" I say, amazed. "He must be good."

"No," replies the nurse. "His handicap is 23. He is very strict about marking his card and is having lessons from the pro."

My only other contact with the hospital golf society was when I was invited to play in their annual charity event. My partner was one of the hospital consultants, and we were partnered by two patients, both as friendly as any golfing companions you might ever meet.

However, as we left the first tee, my partner whispered to me, "Don't get ahead of David," pointing to one of the patients.

"Why not?" I asked.

"He attempted to kill his partner with a club, who had just missed a putt in his club championships.

"What?" I said. "What club was it?"

"A 3 wood."

"Thank God it wasn't a pitching wedge," I said as in that case the word *attempted* would have been removed from the indictment.

"No problem," said my partner, "he has been here eight years and is on a drug that keeps him as gentle as a lamb. But best be on the safe side."

My old leg injury suddenly reappeared, and I spent the round at least 10 yards away from David, although I have to say that the drugs were clearly working as his behaviour was impeccable throughout.

I am getting depressed again, when my downward spiral is stalled by thoughts of Ukraine and, notwithstanding my medical experience, my love for the country and the people. My introduction to Ukraine came about in a surprising and unexpected way. During my legal career, I had met an American lawyer, Jim, who shared my interest in how the management of law firms should be reformed. He was a partner in a law firm in the Southern States of America. He had, by a strange set of circumstances, become involved in setting up a leadership centre in Kiev post-the breakup of the Soviet Union and independence of Ukraine in 1991. The idea was to help bright Ukrainian undergraduates learn how western democratic societies worked.

Knowing of my interest in training and mentoring, having done some lecturing in the UK, he invited me to visit Kiev and give a lecture. I have to say I was initially unenthusiastic. Firstly, I was very busy, and secondly, I didn't know where Ukraine was! I looked it up on a map. A huge country (the size of France) known as the "bread-basket" of the Soviet Union because of its unusually fertile soil, with a history of Russian domination and apocalyptic human suffering during the 20th century. Jim kept pressing me, so I asked him what he would like me to do. "Travel to Kiev and see the centre," he said, "and then go by train to the city of Kharkiv in the east of Ukraine to give a series of lectures to undergraduates, as we are opening a new centre there."

"When will the lectures be given?" I asked.

"6pm," he replied with his usual, persuasively enthusiastic voice.

He explained that under the Soviet system, cities were designated as centres of intellectual excellence and Kharkiv was such a hub with a large number of outstanding students.

I was still not convinced and a further doubt was cast by my son who was at university. When I told him of the lecture time he laughed.

"Six in the afternoon!" he said. "Nobody will be there, and if they are they will either be drunk or lost!"

So, why make the long journey if I am to address a small group of insensible students who probably couldn't understand a word I said? I contacted Jim and explained my lingering concerns.

Three things Jim said:

1. There will be a large attendance. You have to realise a westerner will be a novelty to them. They will have met very few, indeed in some cases, none.

2. You will be surprised by the level of their English and in any event I shall arrange for you to have a translator.

3. Their intellectual ability, although narrow by western standards, will amaze you.

"OK," I said. "I'm in."

I travelled to Kiev and attended the centre. The Ukrainian staff confirmed Jim's third point; perfect English and very smart. Also, delightfully hospitable and charming, if rather shy.

I attended a lecture given by an American businessman friend of Jim's about free-market economics to a large number of both male and female students who listened intently, took copious notes, and asked scholarly questions courteously and surprisingly fluently. I later discovered that a lot of exams at university level in Ukraine are oral.

Following the lecture, the businessman, several members of the centre, some students and I enjoyed a delicious Ukrainian meal in a modest restaurant. The students, aged about 20, remained placid and quiet as if disconcerted by us older westerners. However, when questioned or asking a question, they showed an academic maturity that contrasted with that which I had encountered amongst my son's university friends. They were more serious-minded with glimpses of the youthful vivacity of my own children.

The following day I set off on the overnight sleeper train from Kiev to Kharkiv, 250 miles away with my translator Serge Markarov. We shared a carriage with two bunks. The train was an old Soviet "warhorse" with a carriage attendant who served tea and snacks with the demeanour of someone who knew that they were not going to be the subject of a "customer satisfaction survey".

I discovered my translator, Serge, spoke perfect English, was extremely bright and had a personality that could brighten my darkest mood. He was quite simply delightful. When he smiled, his body smiled. He was funny.

We spent the entire night talking. He told me about his life in the Soviet Union and brought me up to speed with Ukrainian politics (corrupt), and the Ukrainian personality. He turned my lingering scepticism into a mildly eager anticipation.

Kharkiv was a shock. It felt like a neglected town where nothing had been done to improve it for 20 years. There were some large Soviet-style buildings designed to impress by size not beauty. The buildings and roads were in need of comprehensive restoration. One of the key driving skills was to miss potholes that could consume a small car. The hotel, considered modern, was very tired, the room basic and the staff (unused to guests from abroad) unable to speak English. For the first time in my life, I felt isolated. I could not speak the language or be understood or read the signs written in the Cyrillic script.

Nothing in the hotel worked permanently. Suddenly we would be without water for a day, or the lights would fail. No explanation was offered so I assumed it was just one of the attractions of the hotel: uncertainty!

But of course necessity is the mother of invention. What do you do if there is no water for 24 hours? I discovered a cheap answer: champagne! I could purchase a bottle for £1 (very drinkable too) and maintain my customary toilet.

Serge picked me up to take me for my first lecture at the university. Remembering son Tom's word, I had not overprepared and thought, after assessing the students, I would find a topic that might interest them.

The lecture hall was old-fashioned and reminded me of my old school chemistry lab in the '60s. However, shock horror, I was not facing a drunk or amnesiac crowd, but a full house of undergraduates. By western standards, they were dressed plainly and unfashionably. Lots of rather dull knitwear, reflecting a standard of living considerably lower than I had been fortunate to enjoy.

I began to introduce myself with Serge engaging in a breath-taking simultaneous translation. He was so fast that at times I sensed he was translating my thoughts before I spoke.

After about ten minutes, I began to get the feeling that I was not engaging my audience as a bored silence descended on the room. Panic. How to rouse this seemingly unimpressed gathering of some of Ukraine's most gifted students. I suddenly remembered that Serge had told me that my fellow Liverpudlians, The Beatles, were very popular in Ukraine. In the front now sat a young woman looking rather disappointed with my performance. I asked whether she spoke English.

"Yes," she replied.

"Who is your favourite pop group?" I asked, silently praying.

"The Beatles," she blessedly replied.

"And your best loved track?" I enquired, sensing a panic attack and humiliation might be avoided.

"'Yesterday,'" she smiled, a welcome, positive sign.

"Well, come up here and sing it with me," I invited her. "I grew up in Liverpool with The Beatles."

For some of the students who spoke little or no English.

God moves in mysterious ways his miracles to perform, because not only was my invitee a charming extrovert, but she could also sing (as a lot of Ukrainians, I discovered, can) and Paul McCartney's words filled the room to great amusement, and the educational ice was broken. I later learned my partner in "Yesterday" studied Japanese as a hobby.

The silent audience became animated, interested individuals, asking questions about England and how we lived, worked and played. They were as courteous and articulate as the students in Kiev and the following day I told them about capitalism as they had shown an interest in how their system differed from theirs. I gave them some more lectures and got to know the students better. A source of shock to me was how little they knew of the world outside the Soviet Union. It was as if 250 million people had been sealed off from the rest of the world. State censorship severely restricted what they could read, see on TV (if you had one) or even discuss. I discovered that after 1991 a number of lecturers at universities had apologized to their students for providing false historical facts about the USSR and world history. After 1930, English, German and French were taught as a second language in schools.

But, as the vast majority of the Soviet Union couldn't travel abroad, they had no opportunity of testing their language skills. As someone said, "At the end of the day, their English was a dead language like Latin." I was, therefore, surprised by how well some of the students spoke and wrote English.

As the week progressed, I got to know the students better, and we met in smaller, less formal settings which allowed me to get to know them and their histories and to compare their lives with those of a similar age and ability in the UK.

1. They and their families were much poorer, which was reflected in their clothing, social habits, hobbies and living accommodation. Those students whose parents lived in Kharkiv lived at home. Those who lived in other parts of Ukraine either shared very modest student houses or rented a room. Almost the entire population of Kharkiv lived in flats known as "Khruschev flats" which were uniform blocks of prefabricated panels built to house workers in the Soviet Union from the 1960s onwards. They were built to last 30 years but by the time of my visit they had not been replaced, or indeed upgraded or maintained. They were small where sometimes three generations lived, occasionally using a daytime sitting room as a bedroom at night. The furnishings reminded me of post-war Liverpool. A number of students lived with single mothers, their fathers either deserting them or dying of alcoholism. The life expectancy

of a male was alarmingly low. Food was in short supply, but they had developed an ability to cook delicious meals out of apparently thin air, and their hospitality was extravagant.

When I was invited to the home of a student, I would find a table groaning under a miscellany of delectable dishes, together with the mandatory bottle of vodka and champagne, that would put a Michelin three-star chef's tasting menu to shame. Following the required toasts to health, family, happiness, good fortune and whatever else came to mind, I was delighted to find myself in the company of the most warm-hearted, generous, genial and amusing people you could imagine. The more I got to know Ukrainians, the more it seemed to me that we shared a similar sense of humour. Mr. Bean was popular there.

2. The lives that they lived were very different to ours. Born in the Soviet Union, they had experienced the repression of a totalitarian state, although of course they were mostly unaware of it because of their lack of access to information about any alternative lifestyle. As children, they joined the youth movement where they learned to "live correctly" in accordance with Party Doctrine. They told me how their parents would warn them about publicly expressing opinions against the Party, how occasionally a family in a neighbouring flat would suddenly disappear

and nothing would be said. Home became a sanctuary of truth which is why I found the family bonds so strong, in comparison to the growing detachment (particularly geographically) that we have experienced in a more economically mobile society.

It became apparent very quickly that the students were very bright. Their desire to learn was palpable and their ability to learn new facts and theories prodigious. Superior, I had to admit to their contemporaries in the UK. Why, I thought? The answer was simple but qualified.

1. The Soviet system, for all its faults, identified ability, e.g., academic or sporting, early. Those recognised were fast-tracked through a competitive process to the best academic or sporting institutes. One of my students had been singled out in fencing at the age of seven. Academic success also meant a privileged position in society with access to benefits denied one's fellow citizens. Therefore, academic discipline.

2. The students often had academic parents who were themselves intellectual and encouraged their children to pursue academic interests. For example, the mother of one of the students was a professor of English and so her daughter could speak perfect English, but she also taught herself good German, French and Italian. She is now fluent in all the European languages and works

for an international company, speaking in five
languages daily

3. They had fewer distractions. Without money and
freedom, unlike my own children, they spent
more time at home, listening to music and talking
to their parents and grandparents. They had,
therefore, read those books permitted, particularly
Shakespeare, who they could quote at length.

However, I detected a weakness in their academic
approach. They were brilliant in absorbing knowledge,
which was fed to them by their professors, repeating it
BUT NOT CRITICISING IT. They accepted what they
were told. This made lecturing rather frustrating which I
reflected on when I attended a lecture at the university's
law faculty. When the professor entered the lecture theatre,
the students stood, the lecture was delivered, the students
took notes, the students stood, and the professor left. My
game-plan was simple. Deliver a lecture containing some
outrageous nonsense and then ask for the "big brains" to
identify it. After the conclusion and a few minutes silence,
a student said, "I don't think Donald Duck was a great
Russian poet." The dam had burst and my lecture, to much
laughter and enthusiasm, got the critique it deserved.
The number one lesson, I said: "Don't believe everything
anyone tells you. Look at the evidence and make up your
own mind. One word of truth outweighs the whole world."

And so began one of the happiest and most rewarding
periods of my life. I returned to Kharkiv many times, sent
the students books to study and discuss, got to know the

students and their families, and developed friendships that have lasted and they have become like my family. I could write so much more about the years we spent working together and I become emotional thinking about them all grown up now, married with children. They have enriched my life more than they will ever know. I realise it is 3.30am and I am exhausted. I start to cry.

"I always strive, when I can, to spread sweetness and light. I have had several complaints about it."
P.G. Wodehouse

13

Self-Administration of Drugs

Day Seven – Wednesday 7th November, 2018

6.00am   IV. Exhausted. Must have gone to sleep crying.

7.15am   The nurse, who has been a nurse for over 30 years, helps me make the bed with my new bed-making techniques.

"You look like Eamonn Andrews, you know, who did *This Is Your Life*," she says. "You have the same smile. All the greats are dead now."

She told me again how the NHS had become worse during her working lifetime. Poor management, who don't appear to listen and are wholly detached from what is happening on the ward. Nurses are never consulted, and complaints by the nurses are never listened to. I ask whether a manager has ever done a night shift (13 hours).

"No," she replies, "they arrive at 9am and go home at 5pm. They are destroying the NHS."

She continues to complain about the high turnover of staff. Shortage of British nurses means constant recruitment of foreign nurses who may only stay for a couple of years and are expensive to recruit. Therefore, there is poor team spirit. Traditionally, a group of nurses would work together for years under a sister who controlled everything, including the cleaners who were part of the team. Now, the cleaners are subcontractors and report to the management, not to the ward sister. She said that the shift system was too long and made it hard to concentrate, particularly when they were understaffed: "You may be called in between shifts to make up the numbers and have to sacrifice your breaks."

I realise why the doctors and nurses do not appear to be interested in, for example, cleanliness. It's not because they don't care, but they have no authority or control over the contractors, and the complaints to the management are usually ignored or take up an inordinate amount of time being investigated. As one doctor said, "Management meetings normally take a day with a break for lunch and no action plan is ever agreed." Also, the nurses, in particular, feel that complaining may adversely affect their career prospects. It is fear management.

7.00pm   Still on OWL Wi-Fi. Never knew the sex life of

pelicans was so romantic and complex. But a high divorce rate!

7.30pm　A new nurse arrives to run the ward overnight. He has been a nurse for 11 years, and is the senior nurse in A&E, controlling a staff of 10-12 nurses. He is how you imagine a perfect nurse to be: strong, personable, smart, intelligent, efficient, talks to you and gives you confidence that you are in good hands. Loves working in A&E and is filling in on our ward because of a shortage.

There appears to be a shortage of senior nurses who, as Kay says in *This Is Going to Hurt*, provide invaluable experience to help young doctors.

The toilet is a mess again. A dirty towel and a pair of socks remain on the floor. The cleaner has been around but, presumably due to a bathroom allergy, gives it a miss. The cleaner on this ward is idle, monosyllabic and useless, and looks as if he would prefer to be anywhere other than in the hospital. I am reminded that there is a significant difference between short- (up to three days) and long-term patients in their need for a healing environment.

For the last seven days, I have been capable of opening my locker that contains my regular medication which I brought with me. I self-medicate because of the unusual drugs I take at specific times of the day and night for my neurological problems. Today, when I wake up, the locker is locked. I ask the male nurse why this is.

"It is protocol," he replies authoritatively, taking the key out of his pocket, showing it to me and putting it back.

"But I have been self-medicating for seven days," I reply politely.

"Now I control the drugs," he replies emphatically.

"Tell me why I can't self-medicate," I say, getting slightly irritated.

"Protocol."

"Which one?"

"Hospital protocol."

"Can you show it to me?"

"No, it's hospital protocol," he says, treating me as if I were a 10-year-old child.

He has a student nurse with him who confirms that it is the hospital protocol and if he (the nurse) disobeys, he will be reprimanded. "Patients can self-harm or have their drugs stolen," he explains.

"In the seven days I have been here, has any of the many doctors and nurses who have seen me suggested I might be a self-harmer? I keep the drugs well hidden." I am getting angrier and more frustrated. "Isn't the solution that you have a key, and I have a key, and I shall make sure that I don't self-harm or have them stolen."

"No," he says with the look of a man who is not going to engage in a sensible, rational debate.

I am now very annoyed and say, "OK, you show me the protocol, and you can keep the key."

"No, it is the protocol," he says adamantly.

I calm down, realising that I am not going to win the point by getting angry.

I say, "It is my understanding that a patient and the responsible carer, i.e. the medical staff, can agree that the patient can self-medicate if he is capable of doing so. It allows the patient independence and saves the nursing staff time and increased workload."

He does not know that I have been a solicitor for many years.

After he leaves, I quickly look up "self-medication in hospitals" on the internet and I discover the *Journal of The International Society for Quality in Health Care*, 24.03.2018 Policy Document 22 Medication Assessment 2.21 that states, "Some service users," (of whom I am one), "wish to, and are capable of, administering their own medication and keep it themselves. They may choose to do this and people wherever possible should be encouraged and supported to administer their own medicine to maintain their independence."

There are guideline notes for medical staff to make a risk assessment, including discussing the matter with the patient.

Again, I recall Akhmatova: "After a long stay, all hospitals turn into prisons."

I am beginning to feel like a prisoner.

I speak to the nurse again, and stress that I am not trying to be difficult, but an organisation that disregards the rights of the individual and controls by protocol can become oppressive as history must have taught him. We must all use our common sense and, if in doubt, question the protocol and use one's discretion. I tell him that in my life I have had the pleasure of mentoring a large number of young people, mostly professionals and businessmen and women. My mentoring is not based on how clever I am but how stupid and arrogant I was on many occasions when I was younger, making avoidable errors. The most important lesson I learned was that the key to developing our potential is self-awareness, to know who we are and how others see us. I tell him the story about me as a young solicitor. I prided myself on being a good listener and an astute observer. We decided to use video training to improve our performance, which I certainly felt I did not require. To my utter horror, my interview showed an arrogant and self-opinionated bore who failed to listen to the interviewee at all. After the public humiliation of my video being shown to the class, the trainer said that this was the first time in his ten years' experience that the interviewer (me) had talked for 85 per cent of the time! "I had to change, and I hope that I improved."

"No," he said, "you didn't give me a chance to speak."

"But maybe," I said, "I am much older and more experienced in life and may provide an opportunity to learn."

I used this to muse on what might be the problem with the NHS. Could it be a lack of self-awareness? Are members of staff at all levels given an opportunity to see themselves as others see them?

The nurse hears me out but keeps the key. I am exhausted after the uncomfortable exchange, so I reflect on the evil of totalitarian regimes which rule by destroying individuality and replacing it with conformity, and how people like Akhmatova and Solzhenitsyn have recognized it and risked their lives to expose it. How easy, I thought, to slip into a repressive, dictatorial mindset, particularly when we are young and idealistic and have not experienced pain and suffering.

Alexander Solzhenitsyn describes his conversion as follows: "I have never doubted that the truth would be restored to my people. I believe we shall repent, that we shall be spiritually cleansed, that the Russian nation will be reborn."

Sadly, we are still waiting.

Solzhenitsyn, who in his youth supported the Communist regime, felt that his years in the camps were a positive phase of his life as he realised that the system was a lie and designed to crush the free spirit of the individual, that there were eternal truths that we forget at our peril.

So, what should our reaction be to evil in the world? To poverty, slavery, torture, fake news, financial corruption and totalitarian repression? Nietzsche said: "Always ask the question, *WHY?* If there is no morally satisfactory answer, do something to correct the situation, however small it may be." So, what is the *Why* of the NHS? To allow exceptional medical practitioners to do the job they are trained and experienced to do.

In *Do No Harm*, Henry Marsh tells of an experience of having to attend a lecture. It was a MAST lecture, Mandatory and Statutory Training. It is mandatory for all staff, including consultants. Marsh was one of the most brilliant surgeons in the world, one who developed surgical techniques of breathtaking complexity and risk, with often miraculous results. He reluctantly attends the course and discovers that the course leader's previous experience was in catering. The lecturer tries to give him a folder entitled "MAST WORKBOOK", which he refuses to accept.

The seminar was scheduled to last for three hours, and he settles down to get some sleep: "Halfway through, there was a coffee break before we were to learn about the fire drill and the Principles of Customer Care."

He fortunately got called away to see a patient, but he wrote in the book, "I returned to the Training and Development Centre, the PowerPoint presentation now showed a slide with a long list of the Principles of Consumer Service and Care. 'Communicate effectively, pay attention to detail, act promptly and develop empathy.'

"How strange, I thought, after thirty years of struggling with death, disaster and countless crises and catastrophes, having watched patients bleed to death in my hands... moments of utter despair and of profound exhilaration... How strange it is to be listening to a young man with a background in catering telling me I should develop empathy, keep focused and stay calm."

Marsh, I am sure, could run the NHS Trust easily. The chairman of the Trust could not undertake neurosurgery.

While reflecting on the *Why* question, I ask myself why on earth I am writing this journal? The question becomes pressing when I compare my childish prose to Marsh's eloquence. Also, it is tiring when I am already exhausted. Am I developing a form of literary OCD or has my oversized ego taken control again?

I am reminded of the tragic loss of one of the world's great literary classics. Gogol, the great Russian author, wrote *Dead Souls* in 1842 to immediate critical acclaim. He worked steadily on Part II in 1845 and again in 1852. However, he came under the influence of a religious mystic who persuaded him to burn it. A few fragments survived showing the same genius as Vol. I.

Should I burn my amateurish efforts now?

"Those who deny freedom to others deserve it not for themselves."

Abraham Lincoln

14

Medical Equipment Nightmares

Day Eight – Thursday 8th November, 2018

6.00am   IV, but I awake earlier having had little sleep after the locker incident and tormented by a frightening nightmare.

In the nightmare, a nurse arrives to take my blood pressure and other vital signs. The computer does not appear to respond. She tries again and still no response. Another try, but screen blank.

"I am terribly sorry to tell you, but you are DEAD," she says calmly.

"Dead?!" I reply.

"Yes, *dead!* No doubt about it. The computer tells me that you are *dead*. So, you are *dead*."

"But I am talking to you," I say anxiously. "Is the computer never wrong?"

"Never," she says sternly. "It is produced by Medical Equipment Safety First Ltd., the leading manufacturer in the field."

"Didn't they go into liquidation?" I ask.

"Apparently," she says, beginning to lose patience. "The government has lost £200 million, but the Secretary of State for Health has assured us that the machine is foolproof."

Is this a joke? I think. But no, whatever evidence I produce to the contrary, e.g. getting out of bed and standing on one leg, singing and dancing – she is insistent that she must complete protocol form 36/2/B recording my death.

"Can I appeal?" I say, getting more and more concerned with the computer's conclusion and her inability to recognize the obvious.

"The appeal procedure was abolished recently as government statistics showed that there are too many fraudulent life claims which are costing the NHS hundreds of millions of pounds," she says.

I am feeling dizzy and nauseous. "I hope they're spending the money on more doctors and nurses," I say facetiously.

"No," she answers sharply. "They're upgrading the TV system."

"But ever since I have been here, nobody watches the TV," I say, starting to sweat heavily.

"The management think we need more patient-friendly

channels, which will stop patients complaining all the time, thereby reducing the number of nurses required and the cost of snacks and sedatives. According to a £5 million study by management consultants, the Adult Channel and Sky Sports will do the trick. So, back to your demise, she says, changing to mournful insincerity. "I have checked the computer again, and you are, as we say in the trade, deceased. As I said, the government are committed to clamping down on claims by people who are pretending to be alive to prolong their hospital visits and save on domestic bills."

"So, what happens now?" I stammer.

"I will complete form 36/2/B and email the mortuary, and I have to say that the mortician is an artist, the Van Gogh of morticians."

I lie down, trying to relax. Maybe I am dead and being alive was a dream! My brief philosophical musing is interrupted by the arrival of the mortician, looking like Van Gogh's twin brother. Obviously, a talented colleague had been at work.

"Look," I say calmly and firmly, "I think this must be a mistake. I am most definitely alive."

"That's what they all say," he says, smiling and turning away. "I got form 36/2/B which means it's official and there's no going back. But the good news is I can make your corpse resemble anyone you like. I have done a lot of Robert Redfords and Paul Newmans since *Butch Cassidy and the Sundance Kid*," he says with understated pride. "Omar Sharif was very popular after *Dr Zhivago*, and there's always a demand for the theatrical greats like Laurence Olivier."

"I have always loved Robert De Niro in *Godfather II*," I say.

"Surprisingly, you may think," he replies excitedly, "I have never been asked to do De Niro. So, thank you for providing me with a new challenge. I get bored of the old favourites, and I promise you that Marlon Brando would not be able to tell you apart."

I see the Grim Reaper, the Angel of Death and Charon doing a Three Tenors version of "Knockin' on Heaven's Door".

I awake sweating heavily.

10.30am   Registrar Arrives. They normally stand at the end of the bed, but I ask him to pull up a chair and sit down, which he does.

I tell him about the locker incident and the fact that I have not slept because of it. He hasn't got a clue what my neurological conditions are but agrees that I should self-medicate and says he will give instructions to that effect.

The nurse who had kept the key is not on duty, so I tell my nurse for the day of the doctor's instructions about which she makes no comment but agrees that they key will be returned by 12 o'clock for one of my drugs to be taken. I emphasise to her, as I had to the "protocol" nurse, that timings are crucial, and my next dose is at 12.00.

I think I may have become R.P. McMurphy in *One Flew Over the Cuckoo's Nest*.

The Liverpool drug addict lies on his bed, like a silverback gorilla, wearing a filthy tracksuit and trainers. Under no circumstances will he change into a "fuckin' gown", he tells the nurses, and very sensibly they do not argue with him.

A young man is brought to the bed opposite with his arm heavily bandaged. I go over to say hello.

"How are you?" I ask. "What happened?"

"I tried to commit suicide," he replies. "Cut my wrists and severed the nerves."

Shocked by his response, I say the only – crass – thing that I can think of: "I hope you won't do it again. You look like such a nice guy."

"No," he responds, "I am too weak now."

11.00am	Have taken over cleaning the bathroom. Another new talent, although my flair doesn't seem to have been noticed. A crack at the world championships, I think.
11.30am	I go to the nurses' desk to ask if they have a pen. A nurse tells me she is not responsible for pens. So, I ask another nurse who reluctantly hands over a 10p Bic. Another cutback?
11.55am	Locker is still not opened after asking twice. I go into the corridor, look for my nurse and bring her back to the locker. She hands me the key. I thank her. I am a free man again.
12.00pm	Lunch: apple juice, fish pie and apple tart which is no longer dry as I have discovered the milk store and stolen some. Think of the poster with the man in handcuffs.

The Polish chap who delivers lunch almost smiles but quits halfway.

Reading an excellent book by O.S. Guinness, *Long Journey Home*. A few quotes appeal to me.

Pascal: "Man is neither an angel nor a beast, and it is, unfortunately, the case that anyone who tries to act the angel, acts the beast."

"The sole reason for man's unhappiness is that he does not know how to sit quietly in his room."

Certainly one of my problems: speed sickness.

"Unique among living species we live a human life that is aware of itself, yet we find ourselves in a world that doesn't even explain itself."

Viktor Frankl: "We have a fundamental necessity to find MEANING. It is the primary motivational force in man."

The Scouser has his radio on so loud, like a loudspeaker system. Sensibly, nobody mentions it, and I am lucky enough to have sound-reduction earphones.

Water jugs and biscuits are now provided, but I don't eat the biscuits – they are always left. The packets are building up, but nobody seems to want to remove them. I now have enough to feed a small African village for a week.

Return to Guinness's book which I am enjoying more and more. He raises the WHY question again with some thought-provoking quotes.

Abraham Hershel, the Polish-born American rabbi, and one of the leading Jewish theologians of the 20th century, who died in 1972, said, "I only want to answer the questions, 'Who am I?' and 'Whom do I serve?'"

"Evil takes away the WHY."

Viktor Frankl was a Holocaust survivor and one of the 20th century's leading neurologists and psychiatrists, who developed the theory of logotherapy and wrote the inspiring and universally popular book, Man's Search for Meaning, in which he tells the story of a prisoner in Auschwitz who looked out of the window and saw a fat, hanging icicle. He reached out and broke it off to quench his thirst. However, before he could get it into his mouth, a guard snatched it away from his hand and dashed it to pieces on the filthy ground.

The prisoner instinctively burst out: "Why?"

The guard answered with brutal finality: "Here there is no *why.*"

Evil takes away the WHY.

16.30   Tired. Go to the bathroom. Pass the Scouser. He stares without emotion as if living in a parallel universe. He looks dangerously volcanic. Thank God, I didn't ask him to turn his radio down.

He has just been to the bathroom. A mess. Wet towels and socks on the floor, a sink full of facial hair, and the toilet unflushed. He has used my shaving cream. Does he think the Gillette Sensitive Skin Foam is provided by the NHS?

My Slovak friend forgot to put his headphones on, so I listened to a Czech cowboy film. Surprising how you can tell what is happening without understanding a word that is said.

I have run out of paper. On the wall of the ward corridor is one of those metallic holders for brochures to be displayed by being placed in the horizontal sections so that they stand upright. The brochures relate to medical matters incomprehensible to the layman, concerning medical conditions, treatments, safety and emergency procedures. They have obviously not been popular with potential readers as the paper has faded and, rather than remaining proud and vertical, have folded forward like weeping willows, revealing the reverse sides of the brochures.

Should I? Yes, as nobody seems anxious to read them, and having confirmed that I am not being seen, I grab a selection and stuff them down my pyjamas, covered by my dressing gown, and place them under my mattress to flatten them ready for use.

So this is what hospital life has done to me. I entered a retired solicitor, and left a thief!

"Time doesn't seem to pass in the same way in hospitals as it does in other places."
Pedro Almodovar

15

Who Becomes a Doctor... and the Power of a Smile

1.00am   Despite wearing ear plugs, I am unable to tune out the words of my Scouse drug addict neighbour's grievances – "the place is fuckin' crap, the telly doesn't work," and other indictments, all of which contain the word fuckin' which adds to the pained expressions of his elemental, existential desolation. So, I turn to one of my notebooks to seek the diversion of a pithy comic or meaningful epigram. Strangely, I open the book at an extract from a sonnet by Shakespeare
"But thou contrasted to thine own bright eyes,
Feed'st thy light's flame with self-substantial fuel,
Making a famine where abundance lies,
Thyself thy foe, to thy sweet self too cruel."

> *Should I share it with him tomorrow?* I think.
> Perhaps too late!
>
> He reverts to snoring which my ear plugs can
> defend.

2.00am   Can't sleep, so go for a walk.

A Portuguese nurse is sitting at the desk reading *To Kill a Mockingbird*. I comment on what a great book it is.

I go down the corridor to get a coffee. All the offices are only used during the day, but they still have their lights on. No sign of any other nurses, but P is still at her desk, now studying her computer.

"Do you want any paracetamol?" she asks.

"No thanks," I say. "Just having difficulty sleeping. Goodnight."

Certainly no risk of being woken with a pencil light or patients being asked if they are in pain or unable to sleep. I think most patients are reluctant to ring the nurse's alarm, which is next to the bed, unless it's serious.

4.30am   I go for another coffee and ask the nurse for
           another pen, which she kindly gives me. No sign
           of P who has disappeared, presumably *To Kill a*
           Mockingbird.

Van Gogh attempted to become a priest, unsuccessfully, but I read one of his surviving sermons in Guinness's book

"We are pilgrims, our life is a long walk or journey from earth to heaven. I always feel as if I am a traveller going somewhere and to some destination. I know nothing about it, but it is just the feeling of not knowing that makes the real-life we are living now like a one-way journey on a train.

"So, death and even suicide are not the end to one who believes in the eternal home. We cannot get to a star while we are alive any more than we can take a train while we are dead. So, it seems to me possible that cholera, tuberculosis and cancer are celestial means of locomotion just as steamboats, buses and trains are terrestrial means. To die quietly of old age would be therefore to go on foot."

"Sadly, Van Gogh decided it was too slow to go there on foot," Guinness wrote.

I pray that the young, attempted suicide victim, who I gather is a musician, finds meaning in living and goes on foot. What will happen to him when he leaves? Who will look after him, inspire him to use his talent?

The Scouse drug addict seems to be taking the celestial means of locomotion.

11.00am   A young doctor comes to take some blood. I have been trying to guess the backgrounds of the doctors and am getting pretty good at it.

I say I am writing a journal about my hospital experience to help keep me sane. I tell her I am trying to guess which school the young doctor attended.

She looks bemused and makes no comment. I hazard a guess. Either St. Paul's Girls School, in Hammersmith, the Perse School in Cambridge or Wycombe Abbey, in High Wycombe.

My second guess is correct, but my psychic powers pass without recognition. I ask her why 20 per cent of doctors leave the profession within two years of qualifying. She is reluctant to answer but says, "Maybe they just need a break." She brings to mind a quote about one of my school teachers: "She is so dull, ditchwater is thinking of starting a libel action."

After she leaves, I look up Perse School. It's an independent, co-educational, intellectual hothouse founded in 1615 by Stephan Perse. The school motto is "Qui facit per alium facit per se," meaning , "He who does things for others does things for himself." If I see her again (which I don't), I shall ask her what her school motto means. Why are mottos in Latin when 99 per cent of the population hasn't a clue what they mean? How much easier would it be if they were in English? Then the pupils might remember them...and live by them.

I have noticed the older the school, the longer the motto.

My grammar school, which was founded about three hundred years after the Perse School, had reduced its motto to "Ad astra" (to the stars), which most of us thought meant trying to be like Ken Dodd, or the Beatles.

When guessing a young doctor's schooling, it is interestingly easier with women than men. It is clearer where women have gone to a public school than men. A particular style and accent.

What percentage of medical students come from the top independent schools? I ask myself. A high one, I suspect, because the entry requirements are extremely high academically, and statistics appear to confirm that the independent schools produce by far the best results.

Young doctors, in my experience, seem more often to come from medical families who have themselves been privately educated. Medicine is a status choice at A-level. Only the cleverest can consider it, and Medicine is a five- or six-year degree course, twice as long as, say law or history. As I see what I imagine were once eager, young medical students now looking exhausted as they do their rounds, I can't help but ask, how well do we know ourselves, or even have sufficient knowledge, to make an informed choice at 18? A number of young doctors have told me that you get to year four, having lost your initial enthusiasm but think, *I might as well finish and get a qualification rather than start all over again.*

Some people who are destined to be doctors are utterly dedicated to an intellectually challenging and demanding profession. However, how many (as Kay describes so graphically in his marvellous book *This Is Going to Hurt*) qualify, start working in a hospital, in a dysfunctional environment, doing unhealthily long hours, look at their graduate friends in other professions earning considerably more and think, *there is a better lifestyle somewhere else*? Exactly what Kay did by becoming a comedy writer.

A couple of young doctors learning of my life in the law and business and seeing me reading Kay's book have sought my advice on leaving the profession. I always tell them we must follow our passion to be happy and healthy and rewarded. I cite my time on the Senior Directors Course at the London Business School, where three of my class, aged over forty, had been orthopaedic surgeons and one a cardiac surgeon, who had realised that it was not their calling and had become very successful businessmen. The Italian cardiac surgeon was producing vast quantities of men's clothing for sale internationally.

The psychiatrist Sir Simon Wessely wrote a paper on why some doctors become terrorists or murderers: "Motivations for becoming doctors are rarely singular. A wish to heal the sick and injured is one. A wish to have a reasonably secure and well-paid job is another. As is the gratification you can get from the public. But some doctors become venal and greedy. Others become so fixated on science that they lose all humanity. Some become vain and grandiose."

The same applies to all professions.

I go for a walk to the patients' room. Two young physios are trying to help an emaciated young man with a large leg plaster. He doesn't understand a word they are saying and keeps repeating what sounds like "Aylesbury" in a Russian accent. I say I think he may be Russian, having heard the language in Ukraine. One of the physios goes off to see if she can find a Russian-speaker and I chat to the charming physio. "Aylesbury" does not move a muscle. Amazingly, the physio does indeed return with a Russian-speaking nurse who confirms that he is indeed Russian but will only say "Aylesbury". What a global world we live in!

The physios are brilliant with him, but after a few minutes, I leave them. He is still sitting on the bottom stair muttering "Aylesbury", and they are showing super-human levels of patience.

Who is he? I think. *Where does he come from? Why is he here?* I just hope he lives in a bungalow.

I walk down the corridor again. It remains a no-smile zone, with young doctors and nurses glued to their computer screens. What are they looking at? Are they entering required government statistics?

The depression, which had descended on me after so many days in the desolate and often unfriendly ward, is lifted by meeting the Romanian Angel, whose smile immediately melts my cynical old heart. I tell her she always makes me feel better.

She says, "What is in your heart is in your face."

Has to be an angel.

Why doesn't the NHS run a mandatory and statutory training (MAST) course on smiling – to be run, of course, without a man whose only previous experience had been in catering? It would not take long, and need no handbook, just a video of the wonderful Romanian healer.

11.30am   I spill water all over my journal. *My God*, I think, *it will dissolve.* In 30C heat, it quickly turns into a pile of stiffened paper covered in what looks like Egyptian hieroglyphics.

At least my potential readership is reduced to Egyptian archaeologists!

As I watch the pile of cardboard get higher, there is a call from one of my best friends, Peter. He reminds me of my love of poetry, which is true, but for which I lack something in terms of talent, as is apparent from my adolescent ode to my wife. He tells me about a young friend of his who writes poetry and asks if I would be kind enough to read them and comment. "Of course," I say. "There is absolutely nothing to do here for 14 hours a day."

He promptly sends through 20 poems, telling me that she is a young Irish woman who presently works as a hairdresser and has never shown her poems to anybody. Now, I am certainly not a literary critic, but have read enough to be able to distinguish what is good from what is bad. My view is that her work is inconsistent in quality as one would expect of a new writer. However, to my amateur eye, there are lines and stanzas of real quality, which would lead me to believe that she has the makings of a real poet.

My advice is:

- She needs a good poet to mentor her and critique her work. My favourite poet, Wilfred Owen, who was relatively unknown when he met Siegfried Sassoon, benefited enormously from the advice he received from the already acclaimed Sassoon. They were both in Craig Lockhart Hospital in Edinburgh in 1917, suffering from neurasthenia after witnessing the horrors of the First World War

Above all:

- Meet with other poets.
- Read poetry.
- Keep writing.

I enjoyed reading her poems and look forward to seeing her development, I told him.

The heat in the ward reminds me of a botanical garden. It must be the ideal climate for growing the Indonesian orchid, the Chinese flycatcher, or the British MRSA.

The Scouser is a brain-damaged drug addict, I learn. He wants his methadone and is not shy in demanding it.

"What the fuck is going on?" he shouts.

The nurse asks his name and date of birth, then points out these are different from the answers he gave yesterday.

"My fuckin' memory is shot," he explains. "Just get me fuckin' methadone on time."

A new British nurse arrives, who is charming, newly qualified and talkative. We discuss the shortage of British nurses, and she emphasizes the problem of student debt and the difficult working conditions. Although, she says that she loves nursing.

The government doesn't seem to understand why there is a shortage of 5,000 nurses. Removing the student fees would be much cheaper than having to scour the world for nurses.

"Most doctors are prisoners of their education and shackled by their profession."
Richard Diaz

16

A Small Piece of Soap
(...and Back Home)

When I arrived in hospital, I was given a small piece of soap for which I was not particularly grateful. However, its importance became apparent relatively quickly. The soap in the toilet is dispensed from a machine as a light foam. The machine is a couple of feet from the washbasin. So, you pump some into your hand, and by the time you reach the water, it has either evaporated or blown away or produced no lather. So, the small piece of soap becomes an essential part of your survival kit. I think I recall Bear Grylls emphasizing this in one of his survival programmes. It was the one that also included how to deal with a charging elephant, which I found instructive, but sadly have not had an opportunity of testing in Northamptonshire.

The ward window next to my bed is broken and will not open, and we are living in tropical conditions, but I have managed to force it open a couple of inches. However, it will not stay open, so I found a practical as well as intellectual use for the copy of *Middlemarch* I have brought with me.

The Power of Faith

12.00pm   A charming man arrives who is a Catholic volunteer visitor. They must check our admission form. He is warm, friendly and concerned, if rather shy. We have a brief chat, and he kindly says a prayer for me.

I debate whether to ask him to have a word with the Scouse drug addict but decide it might be a bridge too far even for a man of his obvious faith. Also, there is the physical risk.

12.30pm   Silence is broken by the Scouser awakening with the words, "Christ, I'm dying for a fuckin' pee." I pass the bathroom, and all I can here is, "Oh God! Oh God! Oh God!"

My God, I think, *the Catholic visitor has produced one of the greatest conversions since St Paul and St Augustine.*

Later, I open the door cautiously, in case one or two angels are still hovering, and discover immediately that the Holy Spirit has not descended upon the Scouser, but he has in fact been saved by an illicit "ciggy". There could be no doubt, as his cover-up is amateurish. No deodorant smell and a floor covered in ash. I decide to say nothing as am still unsure as to his danger level.

A quote from *Alice in Wonderland* springs to mind: "It would be nice if something made sense in a while."

Charles Dodgson must have written the book during a hospital stay.

Suddenly, there is a cry for help from our resident Liverpool lyricist.

"No fuckin' biscuits! This place is crap. What the fuck!" he cries as if in pain. "This isn't fuckin' right. How can a fucker live without biscuits? It's drivin' me fuckin' mad. It's unbelievable."

His last statement causes me to conclude that he is talking about the Brexit debate.

I put on my noise-reducing headphones and return to reading Guinness's book. I am particularly struck by a quote by a television producer who says, "Our rule of thumb in showing human suffering is that the death of a thousand people in the third world is equivalent to a hundred people in the West, ten adults in our own country and one child in our own community."

It strikes a painful chord; how I have lived my life in a privileged bubble. I remember again the words of Oskar Schindler: "I could have done so much more."

I must never forget I have a *choice* how I behave.

One of the major influences in my life has been Frankl's *Search for Meaning*. I remember one of the most chilling parts when he says, "We who lived in concentration camps can remember the men who walked through the huts comforting others, giving away their last piece of bread. They may have been few in number, but they offer sufficient proof that everything can be taken from a man but one thing: the last of the human freedoms -- to choose one's attitude in any given set of circumstances, to choose one's own way."

Buskers

I have always loved buskers. They often have outstanding musical talent and entertain us and make us feel good daily, without any guarantee of financial reward.

As I look around the ward, at this world I have never experienced before, it is a constant reminder of my blindness to the suffering that surrounds me every day. I think that we all get so involved with our own little world that we rarely take the time to look outside it. There is one man who helped me look at others in a new way, a wonderful busker, Jonny Walker, who sadly died aged 37. I often watch him on YouTube singing "Song for Bernie" about a homeless woman who slept in a bench in Liverpool.

Also, a duet with a homeless man in a wheelchair in Leeds on Christmas Eve.

"Song for Bernie" is very moving and now, more than ever, it comes home to me. The final verse always brings tears to my eyes, particularly as I spent the first 24 years of my life in Liverpool and remember Church Street well:

> There's an empty bench on Church Street where Bernie used to lie
>
> She didn't see the years and people as they slowly trickled by

And left her sitting on her own, beneath the Church
    Street sky
To wait in heavy sadness for the day, the day to say
    goodbye
And it's all right to pretend you don't notice
And it's all right to look the other way
And it's all right to say you won't listen
While she's lying there,
She's the one we just don't see.

I'm pulled away from these thoughts by the Scouser, who is drifting my way without apparently noticing my presence. He picks a chocolate from the box on my window ledge, looks intently at the blue wrapping and drops it back in the box. He looks out the window.

"It's fuckin' high," he says to himself. "No fuckin' chance if you fell from here."

He returns to his lair like a piece of flotsam swept unconsciously by the sea. He sleeps for a while, but then awakens again with the primeval scream: "No fuckin' Weetabix! And my fuckin' telly doesn't work!"

The nurse says she will turn it on for him, but he is adamant: "That fuckin' doesn't work, nor the one by the next bed."

He has been up during the night testing the tellies. He gets up again and is borne my way by some supernatural force and slumps in the chair next to my bed.

"Does your fuckin' telly work?" he asks. "I've tried two and they're fuckin' useless. You have to pay for the fuckin' thing. Can I watch yours?"

Still fearing for my wellbeing, I say, "Yes, of course. I'll pay for it for you."

So, I ring the number required and pay an exorbitant sum for 24 hours. Who profits from this?

I ask him his name.

"Lesley Malone," he appears to remember. "My dad was a politician and me mum lives in a smart bungalow in Liverpool."

I say that I come from Liverpool and ask him where he grew up.

"Bootle," he replies, looking as if he might go to sleep in the chair.

"Amazing," I say. "That is only a mile away from Litherland where I come from. How did you get your injury?" I ask, looking at his heavily bandaged arm and leg.

"Fight with the ex-missus," he says, showing no sign of emotion or resentment.

"She must be very strong," I say.

"She is with a fuckin' machete," he replies. "Special forces."

"I'd stay clear of her," I say sympathetically.

"Good advice, pal. How do I turn the fuckin' telly on?"

I turn it on for him, and he moves the chair nearer the telly, puts on the headphones and goes to the cartoon channel. He looks strangely calm and contented. He watches attentively, except for the odd comment: "That duck is fuckin' useless."

"Run, you stupid fucker," he shouts as the rabbit appears. "The mouse is an arschole."

After thirty minutes, he bends forward, puts his hands and head on his knees and goes to sleep.

Does he dream? I wonder. If so, about what? Perhaps about himself not as a brain-damaged drug addict but a young man with ambitions and energy.

He is woken by two physios who try to get him to walk on his crutches – without success. They are very patient with him and keep trying, but at one point, one of them asks him to try and get out of his chair and onto his crutches again.

"No fuckin' way," he says. "I'm fuckin' knackered."

They leave him, and he goes back to the cartoons. After one last comment, "That Goofy is too fuckin' slow," he goes back to sleep, curled up with his head on his knees, like a child would do. He appears to be at peace, and I wonder what will happen to him when he leaves. So, when he wakes up, I ask him where he will go.

"Back on the street," he says. "I've fallen out with me probation officer since I gave me sister a slappin'"

"But there is a hostel where you can stay?" I ask.

"Fuckin' useless," he replies. "The fuckin' drug dealers wait outside and take any cash you've got. If you don't pay you get a good kickin'. I've had a couple."

I reflect on what a pity it is that the recently admitted drug gang boss patient had not lost all of his head.

12.00pm   I am told my blood results show no infection so I can be disconnected from the IV cannula and go home.

I go to the desk to sign a form. A registrar is on the computer.

"Do you take American Express?" I say jokingly.

I am relieved to be leaving. I think for a moment that she is going to smile, but it turns out to be a yawn

I stay for lunch which is delivered by one of the usual catering staff.

"You are off," he says.

"Yes, thank you for your service," I reply, but he is gone before I have time to finish the sentence.

I use my stolen milk on the dry apple tart. I came in an honest man and leave a thief. Good job I retired as a solicitor, or I could be before the Solicitors Disciplinary Panel.

Day 10 – Saturday 10th November, 2018
Home

I am exhausted when I get home and sleep for 12 hours. My own bed! How I have missed you! I have a relaxing morning reading the paper and finding a hospital story. They appear to be reported more regularly, or did I just miss them before because of lack of interest? The headline reads: MOTHER AND DAUGHTER LIVE ON AN NHS WARD FOR 15 MONTHS.

Apparently, they were waiting for a council house. It cost the NHS £150,000, and 100 patients could have used the bed. The daughter was admitted in July 2017 and the mother slept next to her daughter in a room on a general ward. Doctors said the daughter could be discharged after five weeks, but a new tenant had moved into their flat in

Grimsby. Joyce Robins, who is the co-founder of the group Patients Concern, said their job is to make people better and not offer a free B&B.

Over the following week, I am very tired but also begin to feel re-infected. Go to see Picasso who confirms that this is the case and admits me immediately to a private hospital to have more IV treatment. After five days, I feel better and go home.

A couple of weeks later, I am re-infected and am admitted back into a private hospital. After a further week of IV, it is decided that I need to stay on the IV for six weeks. I have a minor operation performed by a radiologist to insert a PICC Line: a peripherally inserted central catheter. It is a cannula that enters the body through the skin in the arm, into a vein which is then pushed up to a point near the heart. Painless and miraculous, because it means a patient can go home and have the IV treatment there rather than having to stay in the hospital for weeks.

However, I discover that I have to go back to the NHS hospital.

"When life gets hard, try to remember that the life you complain about may only be a dream for the homeless and drug addicts."
Anonymous

17

Return to Hospital...
and Carol Singers

Return to hospital and I am back in my old ward, but this time I am in a single room. Same bed, light, curtains but less noise. For some reason, all the surfaces in the room slope forwards rather than at right angles to the wall, so you cannot put anything on them as it slides straight off. I ask the doctors and nurses why, but nobody knows.

11.30pm   I am self-medicating. Have they forgotten the protocol? Or have they just decided not to engage with the "difficult old bastard"?

My nurse is Italian. We chat about Italy and our love for the country and people for about five minutes. Ten minutes later, I pass him in the corridor without any sign that he might have seen me before.

12.00am   A nurse arrives to check my drugs without any fuss.

Discuss with the pharmacist that I am running out of my specialist drugs. I have taken my last tablet.

Another sleepless night. I am depressed although I know I shouldn't be as there are many in the hospital in much worse condition than me. But I am. I try to raise my spirits by remembering that my medical odyssey began not in the UK but in the Ukraine.

I went to Odessa on business. I had travelled abroad a lot, and there was nothing unusual about this particular trip. In fact, the city was quite beautiful with a significant history and my business associates, who were Ukrainian, were hospitable and friendly. I had a translator. The hotel was modern and, by Ukrainian standards, well-equipped, except that to have a shower you had to step over the surround of the sauna which was about two feet high. In those days, when involved in business here or abroad, I would wake without an alarm at about 6.30am, shower, have breakfast and get on with the business of the day, which I enjoyed.

However, I was dreaming. I was surrounded by people in white coats and under a bright light. I was lying on a trolley being wheeled along a corridor. But it was not a dream. I was actually in hospital, and it was in the late evening. I subsequently discovered that I had, by good fortune, been discovered on the bathroom floor of my hotel room around lunchtime, unconscious and bleeding from a head wound. I had been taken to the only private hospital in Odessa.

I remember trying to speak but finding it difficult. I was placed in a room with another patient in the bed opposite. My translator arrived and told me what had happened, but nobody knew how I had sustained the injury. I was told sometime later by my neurologist in Oxford that it is known as an "unexplained incident" and I suspect that, in my attempt to get out of the shower and jump over the surrounding sauna, I had slipped, fallen and hit my head against some object during my fall.

The initial reaction in the hospital was that I had had a heart attack, but from a CT scan it was apparent that I had in fact suffered a severe head injury and had been unconscious for many hours with concussion. Although I knew what I wanted to say, I found it difficult to form the sentences or to find the correct words. I was told not to lose consciousness again and would be woken if I tried to go to sleep.

The following day, I became more aware of my surroundings. The man in the bed opposite was surrounded by a group who, I discovered, was his family and who were feeding him. In the Ukrainian hospital at that time, you only got the bed and the medical staff, and family members had to buy any drugs prescribed and feed you. My translator brought me some food and said his "connections" would arrange for the patient opposite to be moved so I would have the room to myself, but it would cost money to bribe the hospital administrator. At about 11am, the neurologist arrived. I had discovered in previous visits to the country that, under the Soviet system, young pupils with special talent – whether intellectual or physical -were identified and fast-tracked at special institutes to develop their potential. Of the intellectual students, those who eventually graduated from the top universities were not given any choice as to which vocation they would pursue. The most able men were assigned to "the party" or the army, and the most talented women were moved into teaching and medicine. Some, from both sexes, who had studied law were directed into the prosecutor's department where they would learn the art of accepting bribes to discontinue proceedings against those rich enough to afford this privilege. Thus it was that in the hospital all the senior staff were women.

My neurologist appeared with a group of serious-minded young students. My translator told me that she started the consultation by addressing the students. She informed them that the man lying in bed in front of them was "a western capitalist pig who had come to steal Ukrainian assets and could not even stand up without falling over." This produced a wave of nodding assent and some mirth among the students. She then turned to me. She was aged about 60, slight of build, her grey hair in an untidy bun, she used no cosmetics to enhance her appearance and wore a dark woollen dress and dark brown stockings which reminded me of what women in Liverpool wore in the 1950s. Her expression was void of any empathy, compassion or concern. I suddenly thought of Rosa Klebb, the ruthless KGB agent in the James Bond film, *From Russia with Love*, and, looking down, I noticed apprehensively that she wore the same type of brogues. She had a way of speaking without apparently opening her mouth or moving her lips. My translator rendered her words as following: "You should be dead.",

She announced this with an air of disappointment, and continued, "You have severe concussion of the brain, and you must remain here. Now, put one of your fingers onto your nose." *Time to show you what a western capitalist is capable of*, I thought. But, try as I might and aware that national pride was at stake, I couldn't do it, or even get close. My finger went, strangely, to my ear, eye, chin or any other part of my face but my nose. She turned to her acolytes, said something and they all burst into laughter.

This procedure was repeated twice daily. Other than a rather unpleasant headache and heavy bruising down one side of my right leg, I was not too uncomfortable, thanks to my translator's "connections". Thanks to them I was well fed and reasonably snug with my bedding of "superior quality".

We had contacted a neurologist in Oxford who recommended that I return to the UK as soon as possible as the treatment I was receiving may not have been of the highest international standard. In his outstanding memoir, "Do No Harm", Henry Marsh tells of his experience of going to the Ukraine to help the development of their neurological skills which he found sadly deficient. We contacted my travel insurers who agreed that I could indeed head back to the UK, but required a medical report from my local consultant (Rosa Klebb) confirming that I was fit to travel.

So, during our morning consultation, which normally contained her mantra, "Why you didn't die I don't know," delivered to nods of approval from her back-up group, my translator asked her to provide the report.

She replied, "Under no circumstances," without any explanation, and left.

"Why won't she do it?" I enquired.

"Simple," my translator replied. "With what you are paying, you are the goose that is laying the golden eggs. They will keep you here forever."

"But what am I going to do?"

"Bribe her," he responded impassively, as if it was as obvious as the sun rising in the morning.

So, during her afternoon visit, I offered a bottle of the best vodka which she accepted without comment or physical reaction, and my translator (as he told me) offered her $250 to help fund any research project in which she was involved. She went berserk, telling her attendants that the "western capitalist pig" whose life she had saved thought he could simply buy her favours – she, one of the leading neurologists in the Ukraine!

"He is mad as well as bad," she cried, and left.

This isn't going to work, I thought. The next morning, my gift of a carton of her favourite cigarettes was received as unemotionally as the vodka the previous day, and an increased offer of $500 was met with an even more hysterical response, causing her underlings to move back slightly as if she might assault somebody – anybody – within striking distance. I kept my eyes on those shoes, waiting for the blades to appear.

The next day she appeared alone, and as expressionless as ever. After accepting my gift of a bunch of flowers – Ukrainians love flowers – she accepted US\$1000 in return for the report which was duly translated for and approved by my insurers. I never saw her again, paid the exorbitant bill for my hospital stay (presumably a special rate for "western capitalist pigs"), and flew home via Vienna, where a business partner had arranged for a doctor to check me over before my onward flight.

I duly went to Oxford to see a brilliant and charming young neurologist who immediately arranged an MRI which had not been available in Ukraine.

"You're lucky to be alive," he said, in a tone of relief and sympathy. "Not only do you have bruising of the brain but also bleeding which complicates the matter, and I am afraid that your recovery will not be fast."

It wasn't. It took about two years, and for the first year I couldn't drive or indeed do much at all. My business career was over. I had to find a new vocation. This turned out to be, in part at least, making my body a sacrificial offering to the medical profession for the past 15 years and ending up here at 3am in bed 28c in the specialist surgery inpatient ward with nothing to do but remember.

6.00am   IV. Little sleep because of the bed and the light.
8.00am   Ask about the drugs I requested last evening.
1.00pm   Ask about the drugs again.

7.00pm	Ask about the drugs again.
8.00pm	Ask about the drugs again.
9.00pm	Ask about the drugs again.
12.30am	Very angry and get annoyed with the nurse who has spent all evening telling me they are coming from the pharmacy, which is in another building.
2.00am	The drugs arrive, but I am too annoyed to sleep.

Whether it is the drugs, environment or more probably the lack of sleep, but I am losing my ability to remember things, e.g. pieces of poetry that I have learnt or facts that I know well. An example is the poetry of Wilfred Owen, much of which I have learned over the last 30 years. I was introduced to his work through the outstanding biography Wilfred Owen, by Jon Stallworthy. I found the poetry affected me profoundly in a way one cannot rationally understand. Why does a novel, a painting, a piece of music or a poem cause in us such a deep, primeval emotion? I wanted to read Owen's poetry and to know more about his life and tragically early death. I read everything that had been written about him, including extant letters. I always carry with me a copy of his poems.

He was born on 18th March, 1893, near Oswestry in Shropshire, the eldest of four children born to Thomas and Susan Owen. His family moved several times before settling in Shrewsbury in 1907. He was raised and remained an Anglican in part due to a strong relationship with his mother which lasted throughout his life. He was a bright, curious child with an ambition to attend university. He passed the entrance exam for the University of London, but failed to get a first-class honours needed for a scholarship, without which he was unable to attend. Before enlisting in the Artists' Rifles on 21st October, 1915, he worked as a lay assistant to the Vicar of Dunsden near Reading for 18 months and then as a private tutor, teaching English and French at the Berlitz School of Languages in Bordeaux and later with a family.

I need not record his war record in full, save that he served with courage and distinction and, after being diagnosed with Shell Shock (neurasthenia), was sent to Craiglockhart War Hospital in Edinburgh, where he met fellow poet Siegfried Sassoon, whose inspiration would transform Owen's life.

Although not required to do so, he returned to active service in July 1918. He saw it as his duty as a poet to testify to the pointless, heinous depravity of war. I pick up my copy of the poems in my hospital bed. I quote the unfinished draft prologue he wrote for a book of his poems, should they ever be published:

"This book is not about heroes. English Poetry is not yet fit to speak of them.

Nor is it about deeds, or lands, nor anything about glory, honour, might, majesty, dominion, or power, except War.

Above all, I am not concerned with Poetry.

My subject is War, and the pity of War.

The Poetry is in the pity.

Yet these elegies are to this generation in no

sense consolatory. They may be to the next. All a poet can do today is warn. That is why the true Poets must be truthful.

If I thought the letter of this book would last, I might have used proper names; but if the spirit survives—survives Prussia—my ambition and those names will have achieved themselves fresher fields than Flanders…"

I try to remember the poem "Futility" which I know well, but can only put some pieces in place, like doing a jigsaw having lost the picture on the box. I look it up in the book and must learn it tomorrow or I will go mad.

A feeling of hopelessness unexpectedly ambushes me with the "pity of war". How can we supposedly intelligent and sophisticated creatures resort to animal savagery where we are willing to kill another human being who we can see, and if we had met, may have liked very much indeed. As Owen wrote,

"Was it for this the clay grew tall?
−O what made fatuous sunbeams toil
To break earth's sleep at all?"

Do we deserve to survive?

I am rescued from my descent into despondency when memories of my wonderful Ukrainian students reappear to revive me. As I wrote in an earlier chapter, joyful memories will spontaneously and unexpectedly emerge to subconsciously sedate the troubled soul.

After my first visit to Kharkiv, I decided that the most aid I could provide would be to work with a small group who spoke excellent English which would speed up the learning process. So 12 were selected (six men and six women), and I would visit periodically and discuss topics in which they were interested, e.g., how a free market works (I gave them each a copy of Adam Smith's *The Wealth of Nations* and *The Theory of Moral Sentiments*). They devoured the books, debated how a free market could operate in a country that was endemically corrupt which Ukraine then was and which they had no chance of reforming individually.

The more time I spent with them, the more their potential became apparent. They were not only bright, they were exceptionally clever on any international standard. There were two problems, however. One, they had lived in a strictly hierarchical, individualistic society. You did what someone above told you to do without exception, and teams were not encouraged. I therefore started to get them to work in teams, posing questions in which the group – and not one individual – had to make a decision. At first, they struggled. The person appointed the chairman/woman would basically tell the others what the solution was, without opening the subject up for general discussion. Status was power, and power was not to be called into question. Pretty quickly, they adapted and four or five big brains worked on the problem together, interestingly, sometimes producing a compromise answer that none had thought of initially and which they all felt was eminently fair and serviceable. The power of the team!

The second problem was their lack of confidence.

Because they had not been exposed to international competition they didn't know how good they were. Also, their lives had been mapped out by the state without any input on their part. Others made decisions for them. The cleverest man went into the army or the Party, woman into medicine or teaching. You could not make your own way or dream about being something. To get over this mindset, I encouraged them to pin a large piece of plain paper on the wall of their accommodation and write on it any ideas of what they might like to do in life, however insane in might appear, as our subconscious knows the answer and will produce it outside our conscious control. On the top of the board you write, "Dreams come true."

As they were approaching graduation, I told them I thought they should apply to do a Master's degree in the UK or American universities. This went down like a lead balloon. "Impossible," they would unanimously respond. "It cannot be done for us. It will only result in failure and what good will that do? We are not good enough."

"Well, just try," I would implore them. "If it doesn't work out, you haven't lost anything. Nobody will know, and you can get on with a career in Ukraine."

They wouldn't fill in the application form.

There was one exceptionally bright student, Sasha, who was rather more extrovert than the rest and whose English was as good as that of a UK graduate. He was graduating in law. So, I made an application on his behalf to Oriel College, Oxford. They asked to interview him. He flew to London and I took him to Oriel. I deliberately arrived early, told him that I had some shopping to do and he should just wander about the college. When I arrived back, he was standing almost transfixed and said, "It's amazing. So beautiful."

He won a scholarship to read for a Master's degree in international law which he did the following year. His graduation produced one of the most emotional days of my life. His parents, Oleksiy and Tetyana, lived in a small town in the Poltava region of Ukraine. We decided to bring them to Oxford to attend the graduation at Wren's Sheldonian Theatre, built in 1669. They spoke no English.

We settled ourselves in the gallery for the chancellor to announce that, as was customary, the ceremony would be conducted in Latin and there would be no applause. At the appropriate time, Sasha, who was a large, strong young man, processed in, wearing his dark suit, white shirt, winged collar and white bow-tie, black silk gown with blue poplin silk and white fur fabric hood; at which point the silence was broken by the very soft, uncontrollable sobbing of two immensely proud parents and one elated, middle-aged Englishman.

However, my emotional intemperance was reduced to breaking point when we met Sasha after the ceremony. He walked towards me, tears in his eyes, lifted me up (no mean feat) and said, "Dreams do come true."

If a man could drown in his own tears, I came dangerously close.

It was a glorious weekend and Oleksiy and Tetyana proved to be the most delightful, charming and intelligent couple you could imagine. He was very musical, played a number of instruments and was the town's choirmaster.

Sasha could play the accordion. The benefit of not having a television to watch all day?! They have remained special friends ever since.

While they were staying, a fascinating fact emerged. Oleksiy had told us how he grew a number of varieties of fruits and vegetables, but he and Tetyana did not seem to particularly like English food, including vegetables and fruit. They were far too polite to say anything, so I asked Sasha if there was a problem. What we discovered was that, to them, the items had an unusual taste. After some discussion, we discovered the answer. Everything they ate at home they grew themselves and ate fresh. What they found unusual in our food was the taste of additives which they had never experienced.

Once Sasha had shown the way, other students followed, to study for Master's degrees in Paris, at SOAS in London, at Sussex University, and Sasha's girlfriend Tanya at Oxford. Natasha the multi-linguist got an MBA at ESADE Business School in Barcelona; Oxana an MBA at London Business School and Sasha took an MBA in Madrid.

They are all grown up now, married with children and spread around the globe. We created a club, "The Old Speckled Hen" named because when they came to visit the UK, they had to have a drink of Old Speckled Hen beer.

I am so lucky to have this extended family who never forget me and regularly, for example on my birthday, thank me for my help. I remind them of a simple truth: they gave me far more than I gave them.

I say a prayer for them and their families and go to sleep with tears of joy and thankfulness.

Saturday 22nd December, 2018

6.00am   IV. After such an enjoyable trip down memory lane last night, I wake feeling more optimistic, but it does not last and I am losing the plot again. Will I be out for Christmas?

Tiredness doesn't take long to manifest itself, but I continue desperately trying to reboot my brain and remember the poem. My attempts revive another powerful, emotional experience of my life. My passion for Owen and his poetry gave me the idea of walking with my wife the last few days of his life, which had been well documented, ending with his death as British troops attempted to cross the Sambre-Oise canal at Ors in the half-light of the morning of November 4th, 1918. The crossing resulted in an enormous number of deaths and casualties. Four Victoria Crosses were awarded for that morning's work, two posthumously, 2nd Lt. Kirk and Acting Lt. Col. Marshall, both of whom are buried in the British corner of Ors village cemetery in the same row as Lt. W.E.S. Owen M.C. It was said of Owen that throughout, he remained calm, encouraging and supporting his men, before being hit and killed on one of the rafts in the water.

The journey to the final resting place had been an extraordinary and emotional history lesson. We stayed in the small villages where the men had rested during those final days to discover that recollections had not and could not be erased. Firstly, they could not because evidence of the deadly hostilities was still appearing almost daily in the local terrain. Nature produced not only crops, trees and fragrant plants but bones, bombs, shells, helmets and the name tags of those killed. In one village we met an old chap who invited us to see his "collection". He took us to a small house behind which was a large wooden building which, to our amazement, contained a vast store of artefacts including a German tank

Memories also remained strong because almost everyone we met had lost family members during the fighting, and the war memorials and immaculately kept war cemeteries were a constant reminder. I remember us visiting the largest and most imposing memorial at Thiepval for 72,395 soldiers missing in action. Although there was quite a large number of tourists, it was totally silent, and I recalled the last verse of Owen's poem "Spring Offensive":

> But what say such as from existence' brink
> Ventured but drave too swift to sink,
> The few who rushed in the body to enter hell,
> And there out-fiending all its fiends and flames
> With superhuman inhumanities,
> Long-famous glories, immemorial shames—
> And crawling slowly back, have by degrees
> Regained cool peaceful air in wonder—
> Why speak not they of comrades that went under?

For the headstone of Owen's grave in Ors cemetery, his mother Susan chose a quotation from one of his poems, "The End":

"Shall life renew these bodies? Of a truth,
All death will he annul."

Sadly, and I don't know if anyone knows why, of whether Susan ever saw the gravestone, what Owen actually wrote was:

"Shall life renew these bodies? Of a truth,
All death will he annul, all tears assuage?"

followed by:

"Or fill the void veins once again with youth,
And wash with an immortal water age?"

which he answered in the last verse in the negative, offering no hope for future redemptions. Did she deliberately want to offer hope rather than Wilfred's opposite meaning? Notwithstanding the obvious misquotation, I stood and cried uncontrollably.

Following my recollection of this uniquely special moment in my life, I set about remembering "Futility" and said it every day thereafter, to prove to myself that I was not in fact losing my marbles:

Futility

Move him into the sun—
Gently its touch awoke him once,
At home, whispering of fields unsown.
Always it woke him, even in France,

Until this morning and this snow.
If anything might rouse him now
The kind old sun will know.

Think how it wakes the seeds,—
Woke, once, the clays of a cold star.
Are limbs, so dear-achieved, are sides,
Full-nerved,—still warm,—too hard to stir?
Was it for this the clay grew tall?
—O what made fatuous sunbeams toil
To break earth's sleep at all?

Akhmatova's words echo through my head yet again:
"After a lengthy stay, all hospitals turn into prisons."

10.40am   A nurse arrives to check my medication. I say that I self-medicate and there has been no change since yesterday. However, she insists on reading them from the computer, and I show her each packet individually. It takes about 15 minutes. I don't feel that annoyed. Am I becoming institutionalized?

11.00am   Young registrar arrives, and I tell her about my drug problem yesterday. Doesn't seem very interested. I ask when she thinks I might go home. She says she is waiting for the microbiology reports and instructs one of her juniors to chase it up.

12.00pm   Lunch. No notice taken of the cups left on my table. I ask the server if he can take them away.

He gives me a look as if I was asking for his kidney for a transplant and reluctantly does so.

The sight of lunch depresses me, but I am again saved by the memory of an extraordinary meal I had in Kharkiv at the home of one of my students, Olga. As I got to know the group, I was very kindly invited to have a meal with their parents. I arrived at her home for dinner, to be met by her father and mother, Yura and Ludmilla, neither of whom spoke English. The welcome was the usual, warm Ukrainian greeting and the table reflected the unique hospitality and generosity of its people. The food was absolutely delicious and was accompanied by the usual vodka and champagne. With Olga translating, we exchanged the customary toasts, drinking a small glass of vodka in one shot without putting the glass down.

Yura proved to be a most genial host, a man who I imagined enjoyed a party and he and Ludmilla and Olga (who obviously adored him) laughed and shared jokes.

As the evening unfolded (Ukrainian congeniality is a marathon, not a sprint) and my palate was pleasured to the equivalent of culinary orgasm, the consumption of vodka and champagne reached a linguistic tipping point whereby Yura and I would tell each other jokes in a language we did not understand and fall about laughing.

It reminds me of the joke about a man who goes to prison and as he is trying to get to sleep, he hears a voice yelling, "41!" followed by a laugh from his cell mate.

Then a cry of "33" and another chortle.

"What's going on?" he asks his cell mate.

"Well, we've heard every joke in here so often we've numbered them to save time."

"OK," he says, "can I give it a try?"

So, he yells out, "102!"

And there is uproar. Hysterical laughter, and his cell mate wipes away tears of mirth and says, "That was a great one. We ain't never heard that one before!"

(For more, see Jonathan Silverton's *The Comedy of Error*.)

During the course of this joyous evening I had noticed on the walls of the room a selection of medals and trophies, so I asked Olga what they were for.

"My father was a gymnast," she said, matter-of-factly.

"He must have been good," I said. "These medals in the centre are very striking."

"Yes," she replied modestly, "they are his Olympic medals. He represented the Soviet Union in the Olympic Games."

I was dumbstruck. As a sports fanatic, I discover I am in the presence of an Olympian, and no mention had been made of it.

Reluctantly, he got out his scrapbooks with photographs of him performing those gymnastic feats that still defy belief. He gave me one of him performing on the rings, hanging perfectly still in the shape of a cross. I felt like hugging him in admiration but asked him about his career. He told me that he had been identified as a child and from then on, his life was dedicated to gymnastics. He had travelled to 38 countries to compete but had seen nothing of them other than through the window of a coach that drove them from their hotel to the venue.

I have always been fascinated by the psychology of great sportsmen. What makes them perform at their best under the greatest pressure, whereas I would go to pieces. So, I asked him what was in his mind as he stood beneath the equipment with Olympic glory at stake. What motivated him to perform?

"The Motherland," he immediately acknowledged. "We were bred to think of nothing else."

He told me that when he returned, he was given a small pension, a job coaching in Kharkiv and a more attractive flat.

He was happy that Ukraine was now independent but confused and uncertain about the future as so many of the older Ukrainians were. Indeed, some of the students' grandparents would tell how life was better under communism, show me their ration books and reflect on how life was more certain. They had a point, as uncontrolled inflation had decimated their pensions, reducing their standard of living to subsistence level.

Fuelled by vodka, champagne and in the knowledge that I had spent an evening with the most warm-hearted, generous souls it was possible to encounter, I asked Yura would he mind if they took a photograph of me wearing one of his Olympic medals.

"Delighted," he exclaimed, pouring us another glass of champagne to toast the moment.

So, I put the medal on and, in my alcoholically emotional state, could think only of the national anthem and the Union Jack being raised, and the tears flowed!

The following morning, I overslept, but notwithstanding that well-known "morning after feeling",

I felt so thankful for the previous evening's experience. I had learned:

1. That language and lifestyle differences were not a barrier to true friendship. That whoever we are or wherever we come from we have more in common (far more) than we have differences, and often those differences are superficial and create the glorious, colourful tapestry of the world in which we all live. How boring life would be if the world was made up of only those like us.

As the late Chief Rabbi Lord Jonathan Sacks wrote, "we must never forget we are social animals and social media has caused us to disastrously concentrate on the "I" and not the "we", fomenting blind prejudices and selfish views which are much easier to embrace when we have no contact with those who we judge. Our only constant is with those who agree with us electronically, which encourages the views to become more extreme.

Lord Sacks provides a simple suggestion: "Wherever we encounter the word 'self', substitute the word 'other'. So, instead of self-help, other-help. Instead of self-esteem, other-esteem.

"So, for the sake of the future 'you', together let us strengthen the future 'we.'"

And so, that night it was not "I" meeting some Ukrainians, but "us" becoming friends and feeling the warm feeling that this gives us.

2. Yura had taught me a crucial lesson in life which, in my ambition-driven western society, I had overlooked. He lived for today.

After reaching the heights, he could have felt bitter about how life had treated him. He had been, in Olga's words, "a wonderful father" who was enormously proud of what she had achieved. He saw life as an opportunity to give rather than take. To laugh rather than complain. My life is better for having met him and Ludmilla.

And 20 years later, the friendship and love, without meeting them again, remain as strong as ever, although sadly Yura has died.

12.30pm   I speak to the pharmacist who is sitting in the corridor outside the ward looking at her computer. When I ask what went wrong yesterday, she says that she ordered the drugs and will find out what went wrong and report back. I am interested in how the chain of command works or, in my case, doesn't.

1.00pm   Buy some delicious cakes being sold for a Christmas charity by two charming ladies who smile and laugh at the number I buy. I ask them where they work in the hospital. They don't.

A group of nurses appears singing carols with one of them playing the guitar. I join in which makes them laugh, and I am rewarded with some extra cakes.

The rest of the day I lie in bed sweating. The air

conditioning unit is more complex than a NASA launch module. You would have to have a PhD and the eyesight of a hawk to change it. As I have neither, I remain in the tropics.

I go for a walk and, as usual, find the doctors and nurses sitting in front of computers. Nobody looks up. Does nobody realise that eye contact, a simple "Hi" and a smile have a hugely positive effect on a person who is unwell and away from home before Christmas? However, just as my cynicism and pessimism are about to overwhelm me, my saviour appears.

I come across a young doctor, aged about 35, who is obviously in the newly qualified group. He looks at me and smiles with a manner that instantly gives me the impression that he genuinely cares about me. Unusually, he engages in a conversation and tells me his extraordinary story. He attended a comprehensive school in Hull which was under special measures where an academic triumph was five GCSEs. He left to take up an apprenticeship but had always had an interest in Life Sciences. He signed up for an Open University degree, got a first-class honours, applied and got a place at medical school which he had enjoyed and got good results.

He seems so different from the other junior doctors who have taken the conventional bright child/university route. He reminds me of M, the angel nurse on the ward during my last NHS visit. I ponder whether they are born this way, or life's experiences or good training have moulded them into the outstanding medical practitioners they are. I tell the junior doctor's registrar that they have someone who is outstanding and could inspire young people from unorthodox backgrounds to consider medicine as a career from which the profession would, I believe, benefit.

I see him later and tell him that I am writing a book and am including his story as an example of what you can achieve if you really have a passion and the guts to have a go.

He smiles and says, "I am humbled. Thanks."

I suddenly think what is missing – humility. This should become the motto of the NHS or if you come from a posh school, the Latin, *Humilitas*, or *Servi cum humilitate* (serve with humility).

5.00pm   Am going home again.

"There is nothing noble in being superior to your fellow man; true nobility is being superior to your former self."
Ernest Hemingway

18

Reflecting on My Hospital Experience... and Being a Scouser

Sunday 23rd December, 2018 – Home

Spend the day in bed, reviewing the difference between my private hospital experience and the NHS! They are obviously very different models and, as a layman with limited experience, any suggestions may be naïve and disputable. I humbly offer some thoughts:

- A comfortable bed for patients who stay for three days or more (take the cost out of the budget for posters).
- A dark room in which to sleep.
- A single room for long-stay patients so that their sleep is not constantly disrupted by a screaming

drug addict or our natural nocturnal cacophony.

- Cleaning. In the private hospital, my room is cleaned daily by two people who obviously enjoy it and are good at it. One of my cleaners had done the job for fifteen years and said that she had met so many interesting people. However, clearly this is because they are paid more and managed by the hospital and not by a sub-contractor.

- Time is of the essence for some patients and discretion could be exercised on the timing of surgery. In the private hospital, there was a man having hip surgery. He had been in considerable pain for some time, and his job depended on his mobility. The NHS had offered a surgery date in ten months. He was worried that his inability to do his job may result in dismissal. So, he had paid for it privately, out of his savings. I wonder how often this happens.

- A&E units are clogged up with people with minor ailments which our forefathers would have endured for a few days and recovered from naturally. A lot of doctors and nurses talk of a sense of entitlement rather than of gratitude.

- There are more experienced nurses in the private hospital, most of whom have left the NHS. They have more time for patients, will chat, listen, laugh and generally cheer you up. The NHS must not lose senior nurses. Is this all about pay?

- The food is better in the private sector, although, of course, there is a major difference in feeding the many thousands of patients in an NHS hospital and the far fewer in private hospitals.

- The NHS doctors and nurses should be paid more and more British doctors and nurses should be trained and recruited. The main problem in the NHS, and surely the easiest to fix, is the shortage of doctors and nurses.
- Understaffing and shift patterns help to create an environment where stress is causing too many doctors and nurses to leave and not see it as a long-term career. This exodus became even greater in the Covid crisis, where staff were under ever greater pressure.

How many of us actually spend enough time in a hospital ward to assess the quality of patient care? We all agree that nobody in a civilised society should be denied decent healthcare, but anyone with any experience of life will know that a free service will always be abused. Apparently, 21 per cent of GP appointments are missed.

There is no accountability. Should a small fee, say £5, be charged to see your GP? I watch people in my supermarket spending pounds on a product that tells you on the packet that it will kill you – i.e. cigarettes – or buy £10 of lottery tickets where the chance of winning is slightly lower than being killed by a meteorite. Surely, they could afford a small amount to see their GP. With exceptions made for, say, those on social security.

We have to admit that there is no accountability for our lifestyles. I can smoke 50 cigarettes a day, be 10 stone overweight, causing acute and chronic medical conditions, and expect to receive world-class treatment immediately and for free. People must be encouraged (and financial penalties appear to work in most areas of life) to take responsibility for themselves.

I write with no detailed knowledge, but understand that in some countries on the continent their system is:

- Those below a certain financial threshold will always receive free treatment.
- Above that, the state pays 80 per cent of medical bills.
- The remaining 20 per cent is funded by the patient taking out medical insurance, like car, home, contents and life cover. The insurance premium depends on lifestyle choices just as an irresponsible car driver will pay a higher premium.

Following my simplistic, inexperienced views on healthcare, I find myself thinking a lot about how I got to this point. Tired, but happy and relieved as I am, my youth and Liverpool come flooding back.

Liverpool

The Spinners' "In My Liverpool Home" is the anthem of that amazing city where we speak with an "accent exceedingly rare, meet under a statue exceeding bare, and if you want a cathedral, we've got one to spare, in my Liverpool home." There is a nude male statue over the front of a large store in Liverpool. Unfortunately, but rather typically of Liverpool, when it rains it appears as if the statue is urinating on passers.

I was born in Liverpool, and it was my home for 23 years. I am proud to be a Scouser, a term which I was always told is derived from a traditional local dish, Scouse, a cheap stew made from the remains of Sunday's joint. So, on Monday's, we always had Scouse to eat. The Liverpool accent has a unique sound with unique words. There is even a *Learn Yerself Scouse* phrasebook by Frank Shaw. In truth, I learnt English as a second language. Once a Scouser, always a Scouser. To be a Scouser in the 1960s, with the Beatles in their pomp, was to be a chosen one, and I was a star whenever I travelled in Europe, falsely claiming to be a relative of one of the "Fab Four".

Scousers, like the people of all regions, have a unique personality. Humorous, kind, nosey, and talkative. They don't like to conform or be subservient. Liverpool, like Manchester and Leeds, voted Remain in the European Referendum. The character of the Scouser is often unjustly criticised by, for example, fat, blond Old Etonians who have spent more time engaging with their mistresses (and producing children) than with the people of Liverpool.

The Liverpool personality can deceive you into believing the commonly held (but unjust) view that, as one comedian put it: "They suffer from Onedownmanship, an absolute feeling of being put upon." He is wrong. They are fooling us in order to retain the characteristics which history has taught them, to overcome poverty, injustice, neglect, poor housing and corrupt leadership and the decline of one of the great ports in the world. They have retained an unwillingness to conform for conformity's sake, a reluctance to follow the crowd and a passion for justice as exemplified by the families that fought successfully for justice following the Hillsborough football disaster. Described by Brian Meade in the *Mirror* as "the most resilient , inspirational human beings". Matthew Syed said in *The Times*, "As for the families, one cannot imagine what they have been through. They have shown great courage to bring buried truth to light, a battle that has implications beyond football."

How many families would have given up years ago in the face of institutional cover-ups? Not the families of those innocently killed, who never wavered and refused to accept the lies of a national newspaper and the police. They could sense the injustice and the hypocrisy. My grandfather, who was a docker in the 1930s, would tell me how he would walk to work in the morning and stand in a "pen" like sheep. The dock managers would come and pick those they wanted. If rejected, you trudged home to a damp, cold house, with an outside toilet and in some cases (my grandmother) no electricity and no pay. Liverpool people don't forget that an injustice is an injustice.

University Finance

I was fortunate to have a small county council grant which was insufficient to pay for the lifestyle to which I aspired. To cut costs, I gave up *Football Monthly*, acne cleaner, hair conditioner, and stopped buying new clothes and *Playboy*. The latter reluctantly, as I particularly liked the avant-garde articles by Norman Mailer, John Updike and other literary greats." During my holidays, I had to make some money to survive and to fund hitchhiking holidays throughout Europe in the summer. I had four opportunities.

DELIVERING THE CHRISTMAS POST

At Christmas, the Post Office needed additional staff, which fortunately were mostly students. I would work with the full-time postman on his deliveries, me carrying a much larger bag than usual, and his offering Christmas cheer to his "round". The big day was Christmas Day, as we delivered the post in the morning, and he was generously rewarded with cash for his service during the year. Also, a drink was offered, which my man Stan accepted enthusiastically.

About three quarters of the way through the round, I noticed he was getting a bit groggy as we walked along the towpath of the Leeds-Liverpool canal. Suddenly, he fell to his right into the water with a cry of "fuckin' hell". Because of his intoxication, he took some getting back onto dry land, leaving the bag of post floating in the centre of the canal.

"What are we going to do about that bag?" I asked, panicking.

"Fuck the bag," he replied, digging anxiously into his pocket and pulling out a bundle of wet notes.

"Thank God," he said as the bag drifted towards Leeds.

"The bag?!" I shouted.

"Fuck it," he replied. "I'm going home to change, dry the cash and get pissed over lunch."

So he waddled away, looking like a penguin on a David Attenborough documentary. I was left to walk home,

thinking about how many families in the Litherland/
Bootle area were left wondering why Uncle David and
Auntie Lil had left them off the Christmas card list after
26 years!

WORKING IN A BAKERY

There was a bakery near where I lived. In the summer
holidays they required temporary staff to cover holiday
absences. There was one job allocated to students which
was normally undertaken by patients from a local mental
hospital on some form of social integration programme,
but it seemed to be a source of labour that a sane person
would never undertake. It involved standing next to
an oven at about 120 degrees F and removing bread in
tins, banging the tin against a large metal container into
which the bread dropped, and discarding the tins. The
bread never stopped coming so, as a 12-hour shift wore
on notwithstanding some hopelessly inadequate gloves
and armbands, you would start dropping tins onto your
body, leaving ugly scars. This proved a major problem
when we eventually took off and hitchhiked to Spain.
Instead of stripping down to an Italian-style pair of
skimpy trunks with additional fruit inserted, I sat in the
sun fully clothed, worried that any girl would think I was
an S&M enthusiast.

The other job that I undertook was the 12-hour night
shift packing custard tarts into boxes. My partner, opposite
me, was grossly obese and unable to talk, as he ate about
every tenth tart. By the morning he was like Mr Creosote

from Monty Python's *The Meaning of Life*. You waited near the end of the shift to be blown apart by one enormous, human custard tart!

Another guy in the custard tart packing squad came up with the brilliant idea of printing off a thousand copies of a note to be inserted into the tart which read, "You are Scott's Bakery's one millionth customer, and you have won £1 million."

A large police presence was required the following day to suppress one thousand aggressive Scouse women claiming their prize.

A SAW MILL

In the most dangerous and unpleasant job I ever did, we were in a vast factory full of wood-sawing equipment which spun at hundreds of miles an hour as large pieces of wood were inserted and cut into whatever size was required. The noise was horrendous, a constant high-pitched whine as the machine devoured its victim.

Unfortunately, Health and Safety had not penetrated this particular level of Dante's circle of hell, so all of the regular workforce were stone deaf, and only a small number had more than five digits left.

One employee, Sid, only had one arm. So, after lunch in the canteen one day, I asked him what had happened. He spoke with that slightly off-key voice of the deaf or partially deaf.

"I was fuckin' lucky," he said.

"Why?" I asked.

"Well, one day a couple of years ago, I was standing at the end of the factory, having a ciggy when one of the saws broke out of its casement and flew across the factory and cut off me left arm. I was fuckin' lucky as two feet to my left and it would have cut me into two pieces."

He seemed to be a man genuinely content to be alive with only one arm, rather than burdening a mortician with the job of putting two halves of this body together for family viewing. He had also learned to roll and light a cigarette one-handed.

LIVERPOOL DOCKS

My fourth holiday job was working on the docks. My employment highlighted three major Liverpool characteristics:

- Humour.
- Curiosity.
- A sense of justice.

Humour

Immediately I started, I was struck by the dockers' natural, unconscious humour. They all seemed to be comedians, which was illustrated by their nicknames. I am indebted to the great Liverpool historian Ken Pye whose book *Discover Liverpool* is an essential guide for visitors to this great city.

So, here are a few:

Day-old chick: new dockers.

Diesel: These will…as in "Diesel do for our kid. Diesel do for me, man."

Swan Vestas: always on strike.

The broken boomerang: he never comes back.

The clergyman: never has a Sunday off.

The Coronation Kid: she'll crown me when I get home.

The Surgeon: has everyone in stitches.

The Weightlifter: waits while you lift it.

Thrombosis: a bloody clot who always causes trouble.

Wedding Cake: every time he is asked to do any overtime, he always has a wedding to go to.

Wonder Man: I wonder what's in this.

And my favourite… Van Gogh: whenever asked for something, he shouted, "I've got one 'ere."

Is it any wonder that Liverpool has produced so many comedians? They are all comedians.

Curiosity

During one summer stint on the docks, I was pretentiously reading Homer's *The Odyssey* – again, hoping to attract girls of a more intellectual character. I used to read it on the docks during our lunch break, although I was, in truth, far more interested in Stan's copy of *Big Breast Monthly* and the *Sun*.

Anyway, one day, one of the team looked up from the *Sun* and said, "Wha ya readin', kid?"

"*The Odyssey* by Homer," I said.

"What's it all about?"

"It's about a bloke called Odysseus who leaves his missus, Penelope, and can't get back for ten years."

"Christ, I bet he got a good lashin' when he did. My missus would have fucked off with somebody else! She went to her mother's for a week when I was four days late getting back from the Blues' [Everton FC] match at Blackburn."

The Odyssey became our lunchtime reading. The two adventures they particularly liked were Odysseus being tempted by the Sirens and the seduction for sensual pleasure of Calypso. We heard about Odysseus approaching the island of Sirens where the beautiful girls sing, tempting him to abandon all and join them. Odysseus plugs his men's ears with beeswax so they cannot hear their seduction. He alone hears the songs and begs to be released from his fetters, but his men keep him bound.

"Fuck me," said Diesel. "I could have done with a couple of mates like that last Saturday. A pair of sisters were givin' me the come-on down at the club, and I finished up shagging both of them. If only me mates had tied me to the bar. I wouldn't have felt shit on Sunday!"

The boys loved Calypso when they heard she held Odysseus hostage for seven months by her eroticism and sexual antics.

"What a cracker," Van Gogh said. "Sex on tap. My missus has closed up shop since we had our fifth."

Wonder Man, however, sounded a warning note: "Our Dave married a bird who, before they got married, you could barely get your hands inside her bra. But as soon as the priest fired the starting gun, she changed into a nymphomaniac. Anytime, anyplace, including the co-op, on the bus, before and after work. He had to have stitches twice before he got a job as a long-distance lorry driver to take the pressure off. Fortunately, Phil opposite has taken over, but he's had one hospital admission already."

So, sometimes it's better not to get what we wish for.

Justice

The third quality I discovered about a docker is his innate sense of standing up for your rights and the power of negotiation. The dockers had passed down stories of how fathers and grandfathers had suffered appalling treatment. The management had improved, but in 1966, a docker did not forget and the Dock Workers Union proved a powerful and successful defender of workers' rights and safety.

One morning, I was called into the manager's office.

"Swan Vesta is ill," the boss said. "Can you read and write?"

"Yes," I replied proudly.

"Well," he said, "I want you to manage unloading timber."

He gave me a small notebook, a pencil and a sharpener.

"You will go to Dock F and unload timber. What you do is measure the length and width and record it in the book while the lads stack it onto a palette, which will then be picked up by one of the timber companies and you will give them a copy of your notes."

"Absolutely," I said. "Does it involve any more money to carry the heavy burden of management on my shoulders?"

"Fuck off," he shouted as I headed to the office door, realizing it was not a subject for discussion.

Outside, I looked around for my "team". After a few minutes, my boys arrived having had a hearty breakfast. An unusual duo. One, named Ron, was about the size of King Kong. The other, named Dave, was a dwarf who, on tiptoe, barely reached Ron's waist.

"Pete," I said, introducing myself. I have been told we are to unload timber on Dock F."

"Where the fuck is Swan Vesta?" said Dave. "I bet the fucker's on strike," he chuckled.

Ron said nothing; in fact he looked incapable of saying anything. So, off we set down the docks to find our challenge for the day. About halfway there, it started to rain heavily.

"It's pissing down," said Dave perceptively. "No fucking waterproofs. We'd better shelter in the canteen."

A cup of tea and a toasted sandwich later, we emerged into bright sunshine, but still wet as the lead off the canteen roof had been stolen."

As we ambled along, Dave told me he had been married three times, had five kids, all normal size, and had the advantages of being a dwarf. He laughed a lot.

"You never bang your head, and you can get into Anfield [Liverpool FC's ground] under the turnstile," were two of the advantages he gave me for his lack of height. He showed no self-pity and had a selection of great jokes, one of which I remember:

"A bloke goes into a bar with a bull terrier and a duck. Goes up to the bar, says, 'I'll 'ave a pint of bitter,' then turns to the bull terrier and the duck. The terrier says, 'I'll have a Guinness and Donald will have a bitter shandy.'

'Fuck me,' says the barman. 'I've never heard a dog talk.'

'He doesn't,' says the man. 'The duck's a ventriloquist.'"

By the time we were nearing our destination, Ron had said nothing. I looked down at the largest pair of boots I had ever seen.

"What have you been doing recently?" I asked.

He looked down at me with eyes that portrayed no emotion or recognition whatsoever.

"Knick," he grunted.

"I'm sorry," I said. "Not too long, I hope."

"Eight years," he said, after some time for his brain to process a tough question.

I started to panic and, so as not to rouse him further from his slumber and appear to be on his side, I said, "Presumably a total injustice. Liverpool police are notorious for stitching people up."

"No," he said slowly, the words flowing like huge rocks rolling slowly down a mountainside. "I was into drugs and tried to knife a bloke I thought was seeing me missus."

"Gosh," I said. "I bet he deserved it."

After a long pause which led me to believe the conversation was over, he said, even more slowly than before, "No, me eyes have always been bad, and it was the wrong bloke."

I thought it was definitely time to clarify the situation before going any further.

"Are you still doing drugs?" I stammered.

"No, just a few pints now and then."

We reached our destination. Ron slumped onto a large anchor on the dockside and appeared to go to sleep. Trembling, I walked over to Dave who, as he regularly did, was having a snack, a selection of which he kept down his trousers tied to a piece of string at the bottom to avoid any loss of confectionery.

"Ron," I said, "are we safe?"

"No problem, kid," he replied confidently. "They put the big lad in a mental hospital and gave him electric shock treatment. He's been like a lamb ever since, slow but totally harmless. He just keeps budgies now, and you can't get in the fuckin' house for them."

"Great," I said as the lunchtime hooter sounded and Dave rumbled around in his trousers and produced two fish-paste sandwiches, one of which he offered to Ron whose eyes were still closed and who failed to acknowledge his culinary misfortune. I got out a snack my mother had made and decided on my plan of action. Simple: never disagree with Ron. What he wants, he gets. You never know whether medical science always works or some neurotransmitter in the brain could be reactivated.

We found our pile of wood, which was about twelve feet high. Different lengths and widths as anticipated. I kept my eyes firmly on Ron, who stood like a statue at the bottom of the pile. Suddenly, he leapt onto the top of the pile with surprising agility for a man of his size – a movement totally out of character.

"Wouldn't it be better if I was on top?" said Dave. "If he falls, he could kill both of us."

"Dave," I said firmly. "No! What Ron wants, he gets. So, let's start unloading."

Ron seemed calm as he started pushing the planks of wood to the edge of the pile. A problem immediately became apparent. Dave could not reach the wood that Ron was gently pushing towards him.

"Can't you jump?" I implored.

"I'm a fuckin' midget, not a fuckin' bird," he quite rightly replied.

After a few minutes in action, Ron climbed down and appeared to go back to sleep. Stalemate. Dave got a custard pie out of his pocket and enjoyed the sunshine

"What are we going to do?" I asked.

Dave replied, "No idea, pal."

I'm ruined, I thought. *Demotion, the sack, no holiday in the sun on the Costa del Sol.* Then, out of the glistening sunlight, a figure appeared like Clint Eastwood in a spaghetti Western.

"Hi, Swanny," said Dave.

For it was the one and only Swan Vesta, the Union shop steward.

"What's happening?" he asked me.

"The big lad's doing a great job, but Dave can't reach the wood," I said.

"This," said Swanny, without a moment's hesitation, "is obviously a dangerous load, and we're out."

He blew a whistle and about a hundred dockers stopped what they were doing, walked out of the dock gates and settled into the pub opposite.

Day 1 – Negotiating

"We've had enough of this fuckin' management exploitation, being asked to risk our lives on a dangerous load without proper safety equipment. I'm takin' this to management."

Next day at lunch, Swanny arrived, looking exhausted, and addressed us.

"I have been negotiating with the management all night until they fucked off to their big houses in Southport. They are totally indifferent and insensitive to the problems of the working man. But I am going to fight for our basic human rights. We will not be abused. We are human beings, not machines."

Absolutely right, I thought, and Swanny continued, "The bastards will never get us down. I am going back to continue negotiations until every working man in Liverpool receives the guaranteed safety and the dignity he deserves."

Churchillian, I thought. He left to a rendition of "We Shall Not Be Moved", and I drank all day, rapidly spending my holiday money.

The following lunchtime, Swanny arrived looking absolutely knackered but with a triumphant air about him. We knew it was good news. He drank a pint like a man who had just crossed the Sahara on a moped. His eyes were sunk into his head, had gone as far as a man could go mentally and physically without sleep. His voice was hoarse.

"Lads," he said, "after a prolonged and difficult battle for the decent working people of this country, oppressed by the capitalist pigs, I have negotiated a settlement which

I can recommend to you as fellow comrades in the fight for justice and safety."

Another pint to soothe the voice that had spoken relentlessly on our behalf.

"We're gonna put the midget on the top, pushin', and the big guy at the bottom which should create a better working environment. If the midget falls, I've agreed a compensation package if he is unable to return to work. And we will start work tomorrow."

We cheered him through the many pints that followed. *What a man*, I thought. I spent the rest of my holiday money in the euphoria of victory.

We started work the following morning, all rather hungover but powered on by the fact that the working man's voice had been heard and justice had been done. Dave the dwarf got on top of the load and moved with the speed and grace of a ballet dancer, and the work did not appear to cause any damage to the grocery store in his trousers. Ron was in his element, so strong he could lift two planks at once to a "bonus" level of productivity.

The next day, as Swanny was back, I was relieved of my management role, quite happy as I had found the pressure of unexpected, instant promotion stressful. But I had learned a lot.

I saw Ron at the beginning of the shift and said that it had been a real pleasure working with them, and that I had learned a lot. Dave dug into his trousers and offered me one of his mam's treacle tarts, which I tearfully accepted.

Ron said, "Come and see me birds sometime. I love 'em."

I promised I would.

We finished *The Odyssey* with the lads still debating whether the Sirens or Calypso was the better bet.

"I have heard of the greatness of Liverpool, but the reality far surpasses my expectation."
Prince Albert, 1846

19

The OPAT Team and Back to Hospital

Wednesday 2nd January, 2019

Slept all morning and wrote in the afternoon. The Outpatient Parenteral Antimicrobial Therapy (OPAT) nurses come three times a day to give me my IV treatment. The OPAT team are community nurses who make assessments of patients and advise who can be managed at home and discharged from the hospital, and who needs to be admitted. Also, they administer intravenous injections at home to avoid someone like me having to stay in hospital for weeks. In my case, I required IV treatment to administer antibiotics three times a day – at 8.00am, 2.00pm and 10.00pm – for six weeks. I have to say that they were, without exception, outstanding. Almost all senior nurses who have worked in the NHS, but left because of the working conditions. They work alone, are knowledgeable, caring and, above all, always cheerful – even at 10.00pm on a cold, wet winter night. They always cheer me up and share a lot of their experiences in the NHS with me.

7.30pm   The excellent community nurse arrives, and we chat about my experiences in hospital. She agrees that a large number of nurses are overweight because of their eating habits, grazing all day on chocolates during long shifts without breaks to eat. Another of the nurses (Grade 7) has also told me of her experience in an NHS hospital. She complained to the management about what she considered a health hazard on the ward. After two complaints, she was called to see her manager who told her that it was none of her business. So she resigned.

Day 16 – Thursday 3rd January, 2019

9.00am   OPAT nurse arrives. Very critical of present NHS. He is especially critical of management which he says, "ruined the hospitals". Sleep very badly.

Monday 7th January, 2019

I have not been feeling well, and the infection persists. My surgeon suggests some minor surgery (known in the trade as a "washout") to clean the sinuses and check for any physical reason for the continuing infection.

10.00pm   This evening, before the operation, I go for my IV injection to the pre-assessment ward, which is next to the ward where I will go for day surgery tomorrow.

I tell the two nurses I shall require the IV at 8.00am the following morning on the ward before my operation. They assure me that it has been entered into the computer and there will be no problem. My second injection of the day will be done during the surgery.

Tuesday 8th January, 2019
Back in my old ward

7.30am   Arrive at the ward and ask about my 8.00am IV, but the sister in charge says that I am not on the computer, and she cannot do it without a prescription. She has gone to make enquiries.

I walk up to the next floor for an MRI scan with a delightful nurse who tells me she is desperate to be a surgical nurse.

8.30am   Back on the ward. Ask sister about the IV, which is now 30 minutes late (timing is important!).

The pre-assessment ward where I had the IV is about 200 yards along the corridor, so I suggest I walk around and get it done there as I am on their system and have been there several times.

"No," the sister in charge says, sternly, "you are now an IN PATIENT, and you are not permitted to leave the ward."

9.30am Sister arrives and sets up the IV drip.
10.00am The drip doesn't seem to be flowing as normal, so I call a nurse who immediately spots that it has been set up incorrectly. Fixes it and it works perfectly.

Waiting for my op, I distract myself by reading an article in the *Washington Post* by the distinguished journalist Michael Gerson about Donald Trump. I have long been fascinated that a man so patently dishonest, cruel, criminal, sociopathic, stupid and suffering from serious personality disorders – e.g. malignant narcissism – can become the president of the most prosperous country in the world with a strong, established democracy embracing free speech and the rule of law.

Gerson discusses how we have embraced the concept that being "authentic" (a quality that Trump's supporters praise him for) as an acceptable moral and political philosophy, notwithstanding that being authentic can allow you to tell ten thousand easily disprovable lies, have alternative facts, and attack one's enemies in vile, defamatory terms.

Groucho Marx's observations seem to apply perfectly to Trump: "The secret of success is sincerity and honesty, and if you can fake both, you've got it made," and "These are my principles, and if you don't like them, don't worry, I have plenty more."

I quote the article in full and thank Michael Gerson for expressing so clearly the moral dilemma we face:

"Aristotle believed that human beings fulfil their nature by exercising their reason and habituating certain values such as courage, temperance, honour, equanimity, faithfulness, justice and friendship.

"Authenticity is not on the list.

"Rousseau argued differently, putting authenticity at the apex of the virtues. We are born free but are everywhere in social chains. Being true to yourself freely is seen as the chief requirement of a meaningful, happy life. The worst sin is hypocrisy, being untrue to ourselves. Being true to oneself even if it is being true to our eccentricities – however harmful they may be, e.g., cruel and untrue tweets – is more important.

"Aristotle's view is that a human being is in need of formation. As rational creatures, we must learn to be virtuous through formation as opposed to Rousseau's premise that we become virtuous by liberation.

"The latter policy has been the basis of right-wing philosophy and the former left-wing.

"But now the right-wing have embraced Rousseau as the perfect philosophical fit for an insane president. Or as Frank Sinatra would sing, *I Did It My Way.*

"Here is the skunk at the debauched garden party. If the unfiltered expression of oneself is the highest virtue, then the moral content of that expression becomes a secondary matter.

"Trump may be speaking lies, nonsense or racism, but he remains authentic. It is a shield against responsibility. We hear Trump and begin to believe Trump being Trump, an authentic communicator, even when he lies because the author of those lies is somehow true to himself.

"This is not how we should act.

"This form of authenticity is just the refusal to master the self. It is moral laziness that leads to cruelty, deception and decadence. And a repetition of these failings should not numb us into inaction. Trump is simply a man of bad character, unworthy of respect, trust and high office."

What a gift to write so perceptively and elegantly.
Michael Gerson sadly died on the 17th Nivember 2022 aged 58.

During the course of the morning, I observe my fellow patients. To my left is a tall, young man of about 35. Casually dressed, as if to attend the local Point-to-Point, he is wearing yellow corduroy trousers and suede shoes. As he talks on his phone, I notice that he has a loud, public-school voice and, as it is on speaker, I hear the voice of an equally posh girlfriend. Again, I wonder why people always have to talk with the speakerphone on?

"Appalling," he declares. "I was told I was second

and have been dumped to fifth. It is a disgrace. I'm not putting up with it. I'm going to leave and make another appointment."

When he hangs up the phone, he calls the nurse and asks for the exact time of his obviously minor surgery, as he is a busy man, in "property" which immediately tells me his is a man who has failed every exam he has ever taken and is probably an estate agent.

A middle-aged man arrives on the ward for cataract surgery, which is one of the miracles of modern medical science. A condition that would have rendered my grandparents blind is now cured by a simple operation under a local anaesthetic lasting about 30 minutes. There are 330,000 procedures conducted each year in the UK. He returns to the ward after about 30 minutes and immediately asks to see a senior nurse. A junior nurse arrives and confirms that it has all gone perfectly and he can go home.

"But is there any risk of complications?" he asks. "For example, blood clots?"

The charming junior nurse tries to allay his fears and tells him, "No, everything is fine. Can somebody pick you up?"

"Not for a while," he replies. "The wife is at the doctor's"

"Oh, I am sorry," says the nurse sympathetically. "I hope it is nothing serious."

"She's been feeling unwell and has been searching on the internet. She thinks it might be dengue fever."

"Dengue fever," says the nurse, "is very rare and is caught abroad in warm climates. Has your wife been abroad?"

"No," he continues, "but she was talking to a woman in Tesco's who thought she had it."

"Had *she* been abroad?"

"Majorca," he replied. "But you can't take any risks."

God help their GP!

He continues to stay in bed. The young nurse returns to reassure him that he is fit to go home.

"But I'm still very worried about complications," he insists.

The ward sister arrives. She has obviously dealt with his type before.

"You can go home now," she says, in a tone that indicates she will brook no further discussion.

He dresses, leaves without a goodbye or thank you, and mutters to me, "Is this what you pay your taxes for?"

Ungrateful bastard!

I call the young nurse over and congratulate her on the way she handled the patient.

"I don't know how you do it," I say. "I would lose my temper."

She has a beautiful smile and tells me she only started on the ward a month ago. I ask her if she is enjoying it to which she replies, "Yes."

I ask if there are any problems.

"Yes," she replies shyly. "Because of the understaffing, I don't always get the support I need, and I feel isolated and worried. Some nights, I go home and cry."

I hope she keeps going as she is a natural.

1.00pm   My surgeon kindly comes to apologise for the

delay as he has had a long, complex operation on a child that morning.

"No problem," I say.

"Have something to eat and a rest. I want you in good shape." As ever he laughs.

3.00pm   Go down for surgery.

A very pleasant anaesthetist starts to tell me of the procedure. I ask him if anyone has ever turned back at this stage, and he says, one. We talk about golf and then, as he applies the oxygen, he tells me (as they all do) to think of a place I would like to be. I reply that of the 18, 020 places that immediately come to mind, this is not one of them! I hear his distant laughter, and I am gone to a place nearer death than I will ever be.

I recover slowly from anaesthetics. My experience in private hospitals is that the recovery room is quiet, and a nurse sits next to you holding your hand. Aware that it is perhaps not fair to compare the two, I do miss the comfort of a friendly smile as one returns to the world. At least the Picasso of sinuses comes over as he always does. He holds my hand and tells me all is fine. No problems.

The atmosphere is completely different in the NHS recovery room. As I regain consciousness, instead of seeing the face of a caring nurse smiling at me, I hear the sound of raucous laughter. I can dimly see a group of nurses standing at the nurses' desk, which is in the centre of the room. Sitting at the desk is a grossly overweight nurse telling stories accompanied by a hyena-like laugh. The others join in, but I can't hear what they are laughing

about. My recovery nurse has deserted me to join the
Comedy Store, and as the laughter gets louder, I realise
they are telling holiday stories.

My nurse comes over to check that I am still alive but can't
operate the computer, so another member of the Comedy
Store comes over to assist, still laughing at the last joke.

6.30pm   A nurse arrives to take me back to the ward.

The nurse is charming, and when we get back to the ward,
to reassure me that my life expectancy remains the same,
she tells me that her father is seven years older than me,
did not marry until he was 50, and had three daughters of
whom she is the youngest.

As I am recovering after the surgery, a man enters the
ward. He is middle-aged, neatly dressed, small and slightly
overweight. He has a managerial air about him. He holds a
clipboard with a pen attached. He goes over to the empty
bed opposite, taps the end of the bed, takes a perfunctory
view under it and goes to leave, scribbling something on
his clipboard.

"Afternoon," I say as he passes my bed. "How are you?"

"Very well, thanks," he replies, coming over for a chat.

"Do you work in the hospital?" I enquire.

"Yes," he says, "I am part of the management team that
checks on the work of our subcontractor cleaners."

I tell him I have been in this hospital for over two
weeks, and does he know they employ the world's laziest
cleaner? He gives me the look you would give to either a
serial complainer or someone with early-stage dementia,

but can't work out if it is one or both, or I am making a joke. I tell him that I am writing a journal on life in hospital. At first, he does not appear to understand, but then there is a sudden look of realisation that I might be serious, as I say, "Cleanliness must be one of the top priorities in a hospital."

"Indeed," he replies and suddenly takes on the role of Basil Fawlty in *Fawlty Towers*. He starts crawling under the bed, testing every surface which, disappointingly for him, produces a plume of dust from the top of the dresser. He finishes his frantic efforts, blowing a bit, and says, "All's fine then."

"How often do you do an inspection, then?"

"Once a month," he says sheepishly.

"Once a month?" I exclaim. "To check on cleanliness?"

Presumably to mitigate his incompetence, he rather foolishly says, "But we are under a lot of pressure, so it's probably once every two months."

"Nice to have met you," I say.

"And you," he replies, looking like a rabbit caught in the headlights.

7.00pm   Leave hospital. Difficult as I had forgotten that my bladder is paralysed after the anaesthesia, so I have to stop every 200 yards to release a few miserable drops of pee. By the time I get home I am damp and smell like a French pissoir.

"No kindness, however small, is wasted."

Aesop

20

Home Again and Return to Hospital (January 16th to 20th)

Having received IV treatment three times a day from the wonderful local community nurses, I have been feeling unwell again. I return to hospital to see the consultant microbiologist. She is charming and caring but at a loss to understand why the antibiotic is not working, so suggests switching to another one. However, it requires me to go back into hospital immediately and, therefore, not to go home.

I am taken to the pre-admission ward to await a bed on the ward where I was a patient before.

What happened to the White Coat?
A young female doctor arrives to take my blood pressure and some blood. She is very attractive and is wearing a rather short skirt. She wears sports shoes.

"Your blood pressure is high," she says, oblivious to the fact that a Julia Roberts lookalike is standing next to me.

Another young female doctor arrives in a blouse and trousers. I want to ask them what on earth has happened to the white coat and stethoscope? I am surrounded by the goddesses of medicine, all apparently played by Scarlet Johansson. I try to control my fantasies, partly on the basis that I am being politically incorrect, and if someone could read my mind, I would create a Twitter storm from the #metoo movement. I recall Sophocles' reply when, in old age, he was asked if he still made love: "Good heavens, no! I have gladly made my escape from that savage, barbarous master." I bet he would have changed his mind if surrounded by these "Angels of Healing".

I compare the situation in the legal profession. In the courts, judges and barristers (male and female) wear wigs and gowns so as to retain anonymity and avoid members of the jury being distracted by their physical appearance. If these two were defence lawyers, all the accused would be immediately acquitted.

So, why do the two professions take a different view on their dress code? I am told that the informal dress code in the medical profession is to make doctors less intimidating and to help them relate to their patients. But don't I want my doctor to look like a doctor and not like me, a non-doctor? I want to feel confident that my saviour is qualified and looks the part.

Anthropologists would I suspect argue that we are in danger of forgetting some deeply unconscious (and deeply conscious?) psychological factors recorded by evolutionary scientists like Charles Darwin? Darwin thought that the evolution of secondary sexual characteristics – e.g. the useless plumage of the peacock – can be explained by the different requirements of acquiring a mate. Natural selection will favour any characteristic that helps courtship.

Sexual selection operates in two different ways:

1. Through competition between members of the same sex and
2. Through mate choice between the sexes

So, is female fashion the enaction of a subconscious, involuntary predisposition rooted in a competition between women.

I have no idea whether this is true or not but imagine it to be one of those exam questions that finish: Discuss. I imagine that there would be a wide range of answers!

6.00pm	Admitted to my old ward, but in a single room which my surgeon had kindly organised because of my sleeping disorder.
8.00pm	Have become very anxious, so ask the nurse if I can have something to calm me down and help me sleep as I have previously found sleeping in the hospital bed very difficult. Don't see her again.
9.00pm	A young doctor arrives to take some blood tests and agrees to prescribe some medication. Don't see him again.

10.15pm IV infusion. Ask about drugs. No sign again.

11.00am Ask the nurse whether I can have some digestive biscuits as I am hungry. She says that she will speak to a colleague. Again, never see anyone.

Day 19 – Thursday 17th January, 2019

6.00am IV. Am exhausted after so little sleep.

7.30am Spanish nurse comes and asks me what drugs I am taking. I tell her. She checks them off on the computer and leaves five minutes later. A long day: exhausted. Cannot read, write or dream. Just doze the day away.

A registrar arrives with juniors and a chariot. I resist the temptation to attempt humour again. They ask me again about my symptoms as if they had not read my notes and reports. Or are they testing me as to whether I remember what is wrong with me? Leave saying, "Don't worry, we'll get you better." I find this comforting.

Think about the previous failure of any medication to appear.

Reminder suggestion: a pad to write a request on.

3.30pm My old friend the world's laziest cleaner appears, shows no recognition of my presence. There are two bins in the room, one for domestic waste and one for clinical waste. Both have waste material in them. He presses the pedal on each, the lids open and he takes an executive decision not to empty either of them and leaves without a word.

A man comes to collect the used lunch tray. As usual, I say, "Hi, how are you?" No response, just departs with the tray. As with the doctors, have the NHS created android cleaners and caterers?

6.00pm   Supper. Very tired. Chicken dish with a small tub of ice cream. I get the impression that, since the partnership with Carillion (in liquidation) ended, the portions are much smaller.

New nurse arrives. Reluctant to talk (appears rather nervous!), but eventually admits the nurses are overworked and understaffed.

I am irritated today by the misuse of the English language. I am certainly no English scholar and accept that language is constantly developing and in a cocktail of many ingredients. But now am faced with the fact that words have no meaning or are nonsense, like "alternative facts". I get particularly annoyed by car adverts where a vehicle in shiny, brand-spanking-new condition is driven through a city where there are no other cars, by a handsome young driver and the voiceover tells us to "start a new life". It's a fucking car, and one that, if driven in London, will never go over 12 miles an hour, and will cost you a fortune as you leave the garage. It is not rebirth or winning the lottery!

And people start calling themselves by different names

– e.g. funeral directors are now "The Death Management Industry". Also, on an amusing level, is the Americanization of language. A friend told me of an announcement made during a flight on an American airline: "Good afternoon, soon after take-off, a beverage will be served," and shortly after, "We now intend to beverage you," and finally, "Due to adverse weather conditions, we are unable to complete beverization." My personal favourites are: "This hotel is under-elevatorized"; and to leave being "self-deportation", to have left, "self-deported".

Sometimes, a translation can produce an unexpected result. The French naval motto is: "To the water. It is the hour." Of which, of course, the French translation is: "A l'eau. C'est l'heure."

I always dreamed of being a great writer, until I discovered I had no original thoughts and was merely an ideological plagiarist, a literary magpie agreeing with a better mind…and also, Flaubert apparently took a day to write one line!

We see today, language used as an act of violence through the evil of internet abuse where a pathetic, moronic, stupid coward can hide behind anonymity rather than expose themselves and be revealed as the social pariah that they are. Is it beyond the wit of decent men and women, for example, to ask our parliamentarians to control the Mephistophelean characters who put their personal freedom via the right to anonymity over the death of a vulnerable teenager? How do they sleep at night? And why do WE (the product that produces the vast profits) allow ourselves to be used – for free of course – as parts of an algorithm so that Zuckerberg can continue to suck the soul out of a nation?

Day 20 – Friday 18th January, 2019

Even with a sleeping tablet, sleep badly. It's becoming a nightmare as I wake up exhausted.

6.00am   IV.
7.00am   Breakfast. Ask for two slices of toast and marmalade.
9.30am   No toast! Ask nurse if she can organize it.

Have a long chat with L who I met on my previous visit. She has been a nurse for 30 years. Talk through some of my thoughts and feelings about the ward, all of which she agrees with. She really wants to retire.

I read an article in the paper about Evolution with which I have never really got to grips. Obviously, the description in Genesis 1 of the Old Testament telling of God creating the world and all in it, including ourselves 6,000 years ago is allegorical, merely emphasizing God's infinite powers of creation, even though it might have taken millions of years rather than six days. As Psalm 90:4 tells us in the King James Bible:

"For a thousand years in thy sight are but as yesterday when it is past, and as a watch in the night."

So far as God is concerned, I don't think we need to get too hung up over time.

There appears to me, as someone whose knowledge can be described as at best superficial, a considerable body of scientific knowledge explaining how we evolved to our present state of Homo Sapiens, through a variety of stages, and the evidence must be studied, so young and much brighter minds than mine can reach their own conclusions, without any secular or religious prejudices or the words of a mumsimus. I only added the last few words because I love the sound of the word *mumsimus*, someone who thinks they are right despite clear evidence to the contrary.

In my ignorance, I still find it hard to believe that in a mere 10,000 years, we got from cave-dwelling artists to Dante, Michelangelo, Shakespeare, Picasso, Mozart, Beethoven, Tolstoy et al. To quote the great palaeontologist George Gaylord Simpson (1902-1984): "We are to believe that man is the result of a purposeless and natural process that did not have him in mind." This only makes me wish I had more time and energy to study the subject in detail.

In order to improve my knowledge, I decided to read the work of our leading atheist, Richard Dawkins, *The God Delusion*, which followed the success of his earlier work, *The Selfish Gene*. He had found a large, supportive following which impressed me. However, I found the book disappointing and difficult to read due. Two things in particular caused me problems:

1. The author's vainglorious, humourless self-certainty and lack of humility or doubt, causing me to question the basis of his theory.
2. The lack of any serious counter-arguments, as

if I had to accept the contents unconditionally, which I found rather patronizing, tiresome and unconvincing.

I decided to read a book questioning his views and settled on John Cornwall's *Darwin's Angel: An Angelic Riposte to The God Delusion*, which had great reviews (I am an avid reader of book reviews). The style of the book was very different, offering the reader, without Dawkins' rather arrogant self-certainty, the questions a layman like myself would seek to ask. Cornwall's book allows space for civilised debate rather than a doctrinal view of "the expert".

I liked his gently ironic quotes:

1. "Your book is as innocent of heavy scholarship as it is free of false modesty."
2. "I note that the author most cited (both in the biography and in the text) is yourself, your own works, your own sayings, thought experiments, speculations, conversations with experts and favourable opinions of your work by others."
3. "I loved your admission that Mrs. Dawkins consented to read aloud to you *The God Delusion* in its 400-page entirety, not once but twice. How many professors could boast such uxorious devotion?"
4. "It has been noted that the encomiums on the dust jacket feature of line-up of writers in the realms of fantasy fiction (Philip Pulman), popular brain science (Steven Pinker), an experimental

> pop musician (Brian Eno), and conjuring tricks (Derren Brown). Does this help us locate you within a genre?"

Since leaving hospital I have read A.C. Grayling's *The Frontiers of Knowledge*, which has confused me even more on the subject of evolution, as it is written about things we don't know. For example, after my limited reading, three quotes come to mind, the authors of which I cannot remember.

"Most of the trouble in the world is caused by people wanting to be important."

"The first prerequisite to civilisation is an ability to make polite conversation."

"When man stops believing in God, he does not then believe in nothing, he believes in anything."

My circumscribed research has not led me to a conclusion, but I hope it has taught me some important lessons:

- Don't just listen to an argument or be influenced by the personality of the speaker, but think seriously about the content.
- Find the opposing argument and use the same method.
- Accept that not everything is certain. Doubt may allow new knowledge to emerge or allow time for our subconscious mind to make a decision.
- "Societies' health depends on the simultaneous pursuit of mutually opposed activities or aims.

The adoption of a final solution means the death sentence for humanity," Viktor Frankl.

- "A man does not show his greatness by being at one extremity but rather by touching both at once," Pascal.
- The answer to the theory of evolution is not yet known. Therefore, teaching about it must NEVER be proscribed, particularly in schools. The young and curious (the seeds of not-yet-discovered knowledge) must have full access to the arguments on both sides and make up their own minds, and debate in a civilised way.
- Think for yourself and do not be drawn into group thinking by a false prophet. The fatal dangers of cults over recent years have been revealed in tragic stories of lives being lost or damaged.
- And remember: Love conquers all.

And two final questions come to me as I finish this section:

1. Darwin seems to explain variations and not the creations?
2. In the theory of evolution, where does altruism fit in?

Stupid questions, I suspect, but I will ask them anyway!

12.00pm   Microbiologist arrives and wants to repeat blood tests and thinks I should stay in hospital.

I get a sense they are becoming concerned at my lack of progress.

2.30pm   Surgeon calls to see how I am (he is so kind and caring), cheers me up and says that it is really down to the microbiologists now.

3.00pm   The Italian nurse for the day comes and expertly changes the cannula dressing. She is utterly charming, smiles all the time and laughs. She is obviously very bright with perfect English, and tells me she is going to do something different in life, but won't tell me what it is. She always tickles my toes as she leaves. This is an absolute booster in a world of no smiles.

6.00pm   Try to watch a part of *Les Misérables*, but too tired and fall asleep.

Woken by the sound of the cleaner arriving. He goes through exactly the same routine as yesterday. There is something genuinely robotic about him. Neither the room nor the toilet has been cleaned for two days.

5.30pm   Supper. Apple juice. A child's portion of pasta. Bread roll and cheese and biscuits. Only one small portion of butter for the roll and the cheese. The cream cracker packet containing two biscuits proves impossible to open, and when I eventually rip it apart with my teeth, the 115 pieces of broken biscuit fly off in all directions. I leave some on the floor to see if the cleaner notices.

The piece of cheese – one inch long, by half an inch wide and a quarter of an inch deep and wrapped in plastic – proves an even greater challenge to open. Eventually give up. I think the risk in this ward is not infection, even though that must be high, but starvation. They must be cutting costs after the disastrous partnership with Carillion, now in liquidation. Why did nobody in the government see it coming, as most financial advisors did?

6.30pm   Go out to get a hot chocolate. I get my own and some biscuits. I know where they hide them.

Four nurses standing chatting at the desk. Why not go and have a chat with a *patient*?

There appears to be an overwhelming opinion that the empathy part of nursing is missing. Still not sure why.

7.30pm   Night nurse, ten years qualified. Does not speak much (three children – six, five, and 18 months). Gets on with the job. No chit-chat/empathy. Assisted by a first-year trainee wearing a huge pair of old trainers.

9.30pm   Sleeping tablet.

10.00pm   IV.

Day 21 – Saturday 19th January, 2019

6.00am   Tests/IV.

8.00am   Breakfast. Orange juice, Weetabix, yoghurt, coffee. Ask for toast (*no white, will brown do?*).

9.30am   No toast. Ask a nurse, and it arrives with paracetamol.

Long chat with the wonderful Italian nurse. We discuss what makes us happy. I send her Frankl's *Man's Search for Happiness* and Guinness's *A Long Journey Home*.

10.00am   Another cleaner arrives.

Give my normal greeting, and he responds, "Okay, and you?" He's older, empties the bins, enters the toilets and empties the bin. But then, presumably exhausted, leaves without cleaning the bathroom or the room. Room not cleaned for four days. Are they going for a new world record? There appears to be a record for just about everything these days – the number of raw eggs you can eat in a minute or the length of time you cans spend in a cage with a gorilla – so why not?

4.00pm   My anxiety is relieved by the arrival of another registrar with two charioteers. As usual, she asks me how I am with apparently no knowledge of my discussion with the microbiologist. "I will organise more blood tests and X-rays, and I'm afraid you will have to stay in over the weekend."

Because of the environment described earlier in the book, I found the nights difficult, even after taking some sleeping tablets. Some nights I would write, which accounts for the somewhat undisciplined stream of consciousness which forms much of the book. Other nights, I would walk in the corridors of the hospital, aimlessly passing time and reflecting on the enormous wastage of the vast number of lights left on in unused offices, and feeling angry. Sometimes, in order to try and cheer myself up, I would think of my family and particularly holidays which we had enjoyed. We normally went on our family holidays either in Cornwall, Devon or France, taking a cottage and self-catering for enjoying the local cuisine.

One night I recalled how the beginning of my long and regular relationship with the medical profession coincided with probably our most exotic holiday and the only one in which we met a celebrity. We had booked a holiday in Barbados, when Asclepius (the Greek god of medicine) and Phra Sao (the Thai god of misfortune) had conspired together in an unlikely alliance to disrupt our arrangements. About a month before leaving for the holiday of a lifetime, I was playing Real Tennis in Sussex when I thought I heard a gunshot on the court. It was in fact my Achilles tendon rupturing, which left me with a foot that hung down, unable to perform any of the responsibilities normally associated with that appendage. We drove home and I attended the local hospital, was seen by a charming orthopaedic surgeon who advised me that I was not going home and that he would operate the following morning to sew the rupture together.

He did so with great skill, but the bad news was that I would be on crutches for three months, and the leg would not be weight-bearing, and he said that my best bet was to forget the beauty of Barbados, get a parrot and an eye patch, and audition for the role of Long John Silver in the Christmas panto! However, Felicitas (the Roman Goddess of good luck), dismayed by the work of the Greek and the Thai guys, decided to intervene. My foot and the bottom part of my leg up to my knee was covered in a heavy plaster which, I assumed, prevented me from making a holiday trip. However, the master-plasterer at the hospital came up with a miraculous solution. He said the plaster could be broken in half and fitted with hinges so that the cast could be opened during the flight to relieve the increased pressure on the leg. We rang the airline who, to our surprise, were not only happy for me to fly, but would build a comfortable support in front of my seat on which the leg could rest during the flight, so, with my wheelchair and family, I landed in Barbados.

However, we did discover one or two problems for the disabled in a wheelchair on holiday. Firstly, at that time, local restaurants were not equipped to receive wheelchair guests. No problem when you have a 6' 4", 18-year-old son as strong as a bull to carry you in over his shoulder, much to the amusement and, often, applause of fellow diners.

The second problem was one of manoeuvrability. On our first day I was wheeled to the beach and placed in the shade under a tree, while the family took a boat trip. In the excitement of being in a tropical paradise, we had completely forgotten the work of Copernicus and Galileo, that the earth revolved, resulting in the protection of shade becoming, over a period of time, the glare of the sun. To my horror, I realised that a wheelchair with wheels, buried six inches in sand, was an immovable object, and I was discovered later by my family looking like an over-ripe tomato.

One thing I did learn in a wheelchair, which I have tried not to forget, is that nobody talks to you. As you are three feet below the level of speech, it is as if you don't exist.

The holiday was made unique in that, as mentioned, we met a celebrity. Jeremy Clarkson, of *Top Gear* fame and now leader of the National Union of Farmers, was staying in the hotel with his then-wife. He spent most of the day driving a jet ski around the bay at a speed that created a minor tsunami for us landlubbers. One evening, to our total surprise, he joined us for a drink. The conversation was easy: we ordered the drinks and he talked about himself. Several weeks after our return from holiday, he wrote a piece in one of the Sunday newspapers about his holiday and his fellow guests, referring to us as a "very dull couple from X". He admitted he had a trick to avoid further contact post-holiday, that is, when providing telephone details, he altered one or two numbers, making detection impossible. I thought of writing to the letters page of the newspaper, informing them that I had in fact done exactly the same. At least I could turn the TV off.

So a triumph of medical engineering, an insight into life in a wheelchair, the family who had thoroughly enjoyed themselves, and the honour of meeting a celebrity!

Back in Day 21 and, as noted, even with sleeping tablets I am finding sleep more and more difficult. As usual,

I reach for my notebooks and find, as one always does, Shakespeare, describing the experience in *Henry V*:

> "Oh sleep, Oh Gentle Sleep
> Nature's soft nurse,
> How have I frightened thee
> That now no more will
> Weigh my eyelids down
> And sleep my senses in forgetfulness."

I wonder if he was in hospital at the time of writing?

Day 22 – Sunday 20th January, 2019

6.00am   IV and breakfast as usual. I seem to look forward to the breakfast. Is this a bad sign?

With the day ahead, I reflect on my experience in hospital, and the lessons I have learned as a lawyer and a businessman. The most important one was to treat everyone as an individual. People are like plants. They have to be planted in the right place in the garden – e.g. shady or sunny – then watered and loved. You should treat everybody as unique and not as part of a group. We are special, one-offs, and motivated in different ways. As I say to young people when I lecture, there are 7.5 billion people in the world, but only ONE of you. There has never been a YOU before and there will never be a YOU again. How extraordinary does that make you? In the hospital, new recruits, particularly foreign ones, require individual help from an experienced mentor and not to be thrown in at the deep end and made stressed, and unable to talk to more senior members of staff for fear of appearing inadequate and ruining their career prospects.

In order to have a happy and successful organization, NEVER be understaffed – which the NHS undoubtedly is – with all the consequences that follow. The staff are often too busy to take essential breaks, such as lunch, so instead they graze all day, eating unhealthy snacks and drinks to keep up their energy levels and, in some cases, causing overweight. They are basically standing or walking for thirteen hours a day. From my hospital bed, it all appears so obvious, and I wonder if any study has been undertaken to see how far they walk in a day. I wear a simple watch that tells me.

A search of the internet reveals that studies have found that nurses walk anywhere from three to five miles in a typical shift. Does this explain the lack of emotional contact with the patients they are looking after? Are they just too tired? Is advice given on the best working practices, e.g. rest and diet to sustain them physically for such a long period? Again, there are several websites with advice for nurses, but surely this should be part of their training. Do busy nurses have time to sit down and read this advice in their hectic lives? The staff on the ward are like athletes, so diet and the shift system have a palpable effect on efficiency and morale. I noticed that after about eight hours, the nurses' efficiency and morale started to deteriorate – in marathon runners' terms, they hit the wall.

The shift system is a major problem. Three nights on, then three days off, two days on and two days off, as

I understand it. A minority of the nurses, especially the young, like it as they have the benefit of three days off and can adapt more easily to the disruption of the circadian cycle. The older or married nurses with children, less so. As one nurse in her mid-30s told me, "After three-night shifts, the first day you are asleep, the second like a zombie, and the third feeling almost normal and then next day you start a day shift. However, because of understaffing or illness, you are sometimes called for a shift which disrupts the pattern."

Is it any wonder that senior nurses leave? Resignation and absentee rates are a real problem, but I have never found any exact figures. Do we know the cost of constantly recruiting foreign nurses? I read somewhere that it can cost an NHS trust anywhere from £2,000 to £12,000 to recruit a nurse, depending on where they are from. It is estimated that very soon we will have a shortfall of 10,000 nurses, and that is a great deal of money.

I was told that the hospital had recruited 25 Indian nurses, of whom two had arrived. An article online said that an NHS trust had used an agency to recruit agency nurses, but most had either turned down the job or failed the language requirement. Even using these local recruitment agencies that take a fee for themselves, the costs must be high. Surely it would be cheaper to reinstate bursaries for nurses training and as a consequence have more British nurses?

In order to grow and blossom, young staff must be cared for. Regular mentor sessions allow them to confidentially express their concerns and discuss in a nonthreatening way how they can improve, which they all want to do. Have you ever met anyone who said, "Today I'm actually going to try and get worse at what I am doing,"? The most common complaint I heard from young nurses was isolation, the feeling that if they asked for help, they would be judged inadequate. Training MUST be ongoing, including being listened to, respected, cared for and guided by those with more experience. I have heard the word "bullying" used far too often, but these are people who deal daily with pain, suffering and inevitable death. They are not machines in a widget factory.

Staff should be thanked regularly for their efforts. How powerful! A "Thank you" or a "Well done" is so simple and so effective.

It must be right that those who know what they are doing – i.e. doctors and nurses – make the decisions that directly affect the patient. Of course they need support, but it should be limited to what the frontline staff require. The point is wonderfully illustrated in Marsh's *Do No Harm*. Here he tells of when he was called to a disciplinary hearing by the trust's chief executive for allegedly committing some minor offence when he was, in reality, overriding an utterly nonsensical management diktat which potentially endangered patients.

He recalls, "At eight o'clock in the morning, feeling apprehensive and defensive, I made my way along the endless corridors to the labyrinth of managerial offices in the hearth of the hospital. I passed the doors of the manager and deputy manager for corporate strategy, the interim manager for corporate development, the director for governance, the directors for planning, clinical risk and many other departments with names I cannot remember, a result of expensive reports by management consultants. The Department for Complaints and Improvements, I noted, had been renamed yet again, and was now the Department for Complaints and Compliments.

"The chief executive's office was a suite of rooms with a secretary in the outer room and a larger room with a table with chairs around it at one end and a large desk at the other. Just like, I thought a little sourly, all the politicians and professors I had met in the former Soviet Union."

Finally, I think as I see the disorder around me on the ward, we need great leadership. A leader, not a committee. There is a rule known as the Harvey Abilene Paradox which states, "A group of people together will always make a decision that none of them will agree with." Although, as somebody also said with similar acumen: "A committee is the universally practical displacement activity for people who are not quite sure what they are supposed to do."

Jim Collins wrote one of the best business books, *Good to Great* (which eveyr NHS manager should read) in which he defines a great company as one that survives for, say, over 35 years and not a stock market favourite that crashes and burns within a few years. One of the five factors he identified was that great companies were led by one individual over a long period of time. This leader, he argues, must have certain characteristics:

- They embody a paradoxical mix of personal humility and professional will.

- They are ambitious first and foremost for the company, not themselves.
- They display a compelling modesty, are self-effacing and understated. Less successful companies' leaders have gargantuan personal egos that contribute to the demise of continued mediocrity of the company.
- They display workmanlike diligence, more plough horse than show horse.
- They attribute success to factors other than themselves. When things go wrong, they blame themselves, taking full responsibility, but if they go well, they recognise others.
- They attribute much of their success to good luck, rather than personal greatness.
- They are fanatically driven.
- They stick around through thick and thin.
- They set the highest moral standards. Collins says that the role of the virtuous leader, to paraphrase Aristotle, is "to provide the goods and services a society needs in an economically efficient manner while at the same time providing the environment for the intellectual and moral development of employees."
- They believe that WORK needs to be organised, that THINGS should be MANAGED, but that PEOPLE can only be encouraged, inspired and LED. By things I mean the buildings, information systems or anything physical.

They DON'T, if things go wrong, whether through laziness, incompetence or some moral failing, get a substantial pay-off and increased funding for their pension and sign a non-disclosure agreement. How angry do we get when we see this happen in the NHS? If you fail, you move on to another trust, presumably to take your unique set of skills with you. Why do we pay the chief executive of an NHS trust more than the prime minister or an outstanding consultant?

Do we recognise this type of leadership in the NHS? Or are they an army of bureaucrats, confirming the truth of the Harvey Abilene Paradox?

In summary, a great leader's role is to provide a society with the goods and services it needs in an economically efficient manner while at the same time providing the environment for the intellectual and moral development of employees. I am sure that we can think of a number of leaders whose behaviour is amoral and would thus benefit significantly from applying this.

Don't think you are responsible for your success. True greatness is found in humility. Truly great people are truly humble. Humble people don't think less of themselves, they just think of themselves less. They develop a healthy sense of self-knowledge. Knowing ourselves is the ability to laugh at our perceived self-importance, or our fleeting sense of superiority.

At noon, a wheelchair appears next to my bed, accompanied by a nurse and a porter. The nurse, who I have not seen before, introduces neither herself nor the porter. I introduce myself and ask her what her name is. She replies, with a look as if I had asked her to take her clothes off. We will call her T.

"You are going to the X-ray department," she says.

"But I have walked around the hospital for days, including a trip to the X-ray department, which is one floor above the ward," I insist. "I'll just walk up and save you and the porter's time."

I assume logic will prevail.

"No," she says, giving me the Miss Jean Brodie look.

"Why not?" I say, weak but still desperate for common sense to win the day.

"Protocol," she replies, as if quoting from the Ten Commandments.

"Protocol?" I say. "We are in *Alice in Wonderland*."

She doesn't get it, and I am a beaten man unable to engage in a debate or ask to see the Protocol. They have won, so I leap up and get onto the wheelchair one-legged.

Off I go, pushed by a man who looks like he should be in the chair with – or instead of – me. We travel along empty corridors to the lift and up to our destination. En route, I ask him how long he has been doing the job and if he enjoys it.

"16 years, and no, I need the money," he mutters.

"You must keep very fit?" I repeat several times.

He doesn't seem to understand the question, or maybe confinement has affected my speech.

"Yes, keeps me very fit," he says eventually.

I am parked up in the X-ray department. As there is nobody in sight, I seize the opportunity to stretch my legs and examine the posters and notices which almost completely cover the walls. I am reminded again of the trust's policies and aims to make my stay in hospital as agreeable as possible, how to clean my hands and, as throughout the hospital, the largest poster warns me of the consequences of abusing a member of staff.

After the X-ray is conducted by a delightful young radiologist, I walk up and down until another porter arrives to take me back. I consider walking back but realise it could cause administrative chaos, requiring a "lost patient and a disciplinary hearing for the porter". He finally arrives and we make the journey back to my ward.

I ask again if he enjoys the job as it must keep him fit. He is quite elderly.

"No," he responds gloomily. "Sometimes we work 15-hour shifts."

On return to the ward, the Italian nurse M arrives with her big smile and exuberance, to tell me that the results of the latest blood tests and X-ray are OK, and I can go home. She is like sunlight.

Later, it is confirmed that I am indeed going home, and I am given an envelope full of forms for my GP and the community nursing team. As usual, I open the envelope to check the contents. There are five mistakes which I correct.

I wait for my antibiotics to take home, and a registrar arrives with S, my inspirational doctor. I tell her they must look after him, and she agrees. He smiles shyly and looks as if my going home is the best thing that has happened to him for months.

"Good luck," he says.

"And to you," I reply. "Don't let the bastards grind you down. You are exceptional."

He blushes.

6.00pm   Supper. Vegetable tart.

I am released to complete the IV treatment in the comfort of my own home with the wonderful community nurses.

The following morning there is a headline in the newspaper: "Surgeons Argue During Robotic Heart Surgery."

The article says: "The robot surgery victim died. The lead surgeon said he had not undertaken the procedure before as he had to miss a number of training courses. A furious argument developed before they abandoned the robotic technique and reverted to conventional surgery, but it was too late to save the patient. Prof David Anderson, a consultant cardiac surgeon, brought in by the police to write a report on what went wrong, said 'the victim would have had a 99% chance of survival'. Two doctors, supervising experts, who should be trained to take over if an operation goes wrong, walked out midway through the operation. Prof Anderson said, 'They were not registered with the GMS and therefore not qualified to intervene.'"

Did they not think of waking the patient up and giving him the casting vote?!

I have been at home a couple of days and am rereading my journal. Have I been too hard on the NHS? A danger of discussing the NHS is that it is an organisation and not a person. So, it is essential to distinguish the organisation (employers) from the people who work in it (employees). The fact that the medical staff are outstanding does not mean that the organisation is outstanding. The two are entirely different. It was only one ward in one hospital and therefore had no general validity. I am a trained lawyer, so am I too objective, as lawyers are trained to be?

I sometimes wonder if I had too quaint a picture of the NHS. Was I subconsciously influenced by youthful viewings of *Doctor in the House*, *Dr Kildare* and *Carry on Matron*? Or am I just a grumpy old fart, critical of anything less than perfect? I thought that a good way of answering my questions and doubts was to get hold of a copy of the NHS's Trust Annual Report. I am now on suicide report. It is over 121 pages long.

Amazon, the largest company in the world, has a report of just 76 pages, and they have to earn their money – it is not given to them by the government. The NHS report is very expensively produced. I have spent time in the printing industry, and the contents are a cross between the Berlin telephone directory and the predictions of Nostradamus. I won't go into details – otherwise, I would have to increase my medication – but it is essentially unreadable, and the financial information is produced in a way that would test Warren Buffett, written, no doubt, by a team of expensive management consultants on expensive paper. I ask myself how many copies are produced and how many people read it? Will they tell us? Is the information available under the Data Information legislation?

How many people have read it? The directors, some civil servants, a few politicians? I would hazard a guess the number is in single figures. And how many copies were printed? At what cost? Therefore, what is the cost per reader? The price of an original copy of one of Shakespeare's plays? As I read, I again ask myself, how much time have any of them spent in the actual wards, done the nightshift? How many nights have they slept in a hospital bed? How many times have they washed their hands in the bathroom, tried to sleep without any curtains and surrounded by noise? How many of them actually have private health insurance? The agenda and minutes of board meetings should be available to the public as well as to all staff members – redacting, of course, any particularly sensitive matters.

Have you read your local NHS trust annual report? If so, let me know.

My brilliant surgeon tells me that he is having a battle to obtain a vital piece of equipment for his department without which patients' treatment would be compromised. I'd bet the cost of the annual report would cover the cost comfortably.

With the Pandemic of 2020 (and beyond), the situation must be very different now. From what I can see in the papers, it is even worse, with staff being worked to exhaustion and more nurses leaving than ever.

"There is no nonsense so arrant that it cannot be made the creed of the vast majority by adequate governmental action."
Bertrand Russell

21

Liverpool, My Career Prospects

Now I am back home, I am very tired and drift again into the dreamy half-sleep. I recall my return to Liverpool after university. Strangely, I think of Lesley Malone again, and the young musician, and wonder what has happened to them.

I returned home from university, heavily in debt, and with a dismal academic record. Unemployed, but with that misguided optimism of youth, I was confident that fame and fortune awaited me. But, what to do? The law had not seduced me as my wife had done, but I had no other qualification. Was it back to the docks or the bakery to avoid bankruptcy? No, my only option was the practice of law. Maybe I had underestimated her, seen only her cheerless, uninspiring exterior and missed her inner beauty and intrigue.

With my mother's proven literary ability, we wrote to twenty firms in Liverpool. In her eyes, my talents had blossomed even more, and my musical, social, charitable and sporting achievements were considerably enhanced. My new-found interest in "The Law of Property Act 1925" had to be a clincher.

I got two replies. "Two," my mother explained in triumph, particularly as one was from a leading firm in the city, the other a firm I had never heard of.

With my new suit, shirt, tie, and shoes polished to army standard, I attended an interview with the latter first.

I turned up at this sole solicitor firm to find the office comprised of one very large room in the Victorian style. Sitting in the centre of the room on a raised platform was the principal, presumably like Mr Scrooge, to keep an eye on the employees' productivity and shout instructions to them. The temperature was kept low with most of the staff wearing overcoats. Typists, on old-fashioned typewriters, noisily typed, while clerks (now legal executives) scribbled away, some still hand-writing deeds on vellum.

My potential employer indicated that I could sit and pointed to a chair some feet below him. As I nervously sat down, I noticed first of all that the chair had only one armrest, and part of the seat was missing with some springs exposed, and secondly that, as I was 13st. 7 lb. at the time, the chair was not going to take my full weight. So, I adopted an awkward, semi-squat position, so as not to put all of my weight on the chair.

"What are you?" he yelled down from his celestial seat, leaning forward so I could see his face.

"A graduate," I replied.

"You must remember the solicitor's profession was not an all-graduate profession then, and most solicitors did five-year articles in family firms, who expected a premium for the privilege of joining them or at best provided a modest salary. My future guide to the mysteries of the law had disappeared over the horizon back into his seat and suddenly erupted in a high-pitched laugh which was quickly copied by his staff. After a minute or two, the laughter subsided, and he reappeared over the front of his desk.

"A graduate! What use is a bloody graduate to me?" However, as an act of charity, he added, "I'll give you £1 a week."

I realised that this was not going to be a winner and asked if I could think about it. The final embarrassment was that my squat training was not enough, and the chair collapsed beneath me. I could still hear the laughter as I stood in the street outside the building. Anyway, another chance beckoned from a leading firm in the city.

I arrived at the interview even smarter than the first, having added a new shirt with a detachable, starched collar and tie that might give the impression that I was an alumnus of one of Britain's great public schools (it was very much a public school profession).

The offices were palatial – Georgian furniture, portraits of former partners, the smell of success. "This is where you were meant to be," as my ever-supportive mother said as I left home. I was ushered into a large board room with an enormous mahogany desk where three elderly gentlemen sat, dressed immaculately in beautifully tailored three-piece suits.

It was obvious that they hadn't read my CV because the gentleman in the middle pulled out the document and handed copies to the other two. They all studied the CV for about a minute and then the senior partner asked, "Waterloo Grammar School?"

"Yes," I replied.

"We'll be in touch," he said with the voice of an upper-class undertaker.

Surprisingly, I never heard from them.

The law had jilted me again. My original view was correct: the law is an ass! Particularly not to spot my obvious talent.

The bank wrote to me to advise me that my account was closed, and exorbitant monthly repayments were required. So, it was the docks or the bakery. The sawmill was out of the question. I might have been broke, but remaining a ten-digit man was, I though, crucial.

"Friends, yesterday we stood at the edge of the abyss, but today we have taken a great step forward"

Russian politician addressing his fellow parliamentarians.

22

Send in the Clown

On lunchtime soon after my return home, I got talking to a guy in the pub I frequented, who always seemed to be flush with cash and enquired what I did.

"A comedian," he replied, which surprised me as he never told a joke and seemed rather depressed.

Now, remember this is Liverpool 1968, the centre of the cultural universe. The Beatles, the Mersey Poets, the Everyman Theatre, young, exciting playwrights and of course COMEDY following in the great tradition of Liverpool comics.

I told him that I had done a bit of after-dinner speaking.

"And you're still alive?" he said. "You must be useful."

I wasn't sure whether that was a joke.

"You can help me out, pal," he said. "I've got a double-booking next Thursday. Could you do one for me? It's an easy gig. I'm a regular."

"I better check my diary and speak to my manager,"

I said, hoping to give the impression that I was a real pro and worth a decent fee.

"Give me a ring tomorrow," he said, taking out a fiver and buying me drinks all night.

I rang the next day to say that I was free, but that my manager was concerned about the fee.

"Ten pounds," he said.

I was speechless, which must have led him to believe that I was thinking about it.

"OK, twenty quid."

This was as much as I had earned in a week before and it was for one night only.

"Great," I stammered and, shaking, wrote down the address of the club.

"Next Thursday. Be there at 7," he said, ringing off.

My God, I thought, *this is the opportunity of a lifetime.*

My mother dissolved into tears when I told her, and mouthed, "You always were a funny baby."

The following day, I looked up the address. It appeared to be part of the university, so I started to think about my script. Intellectual satire, irony, mockery, and a parody of student life, I decided, having experienced it myself.

After days and nights of work, and avoiding the pub, I came up with an adaptation of T.S. Eliot's *The Wasteland* as a caricature of Liverpool student life.

Steve, my mate in the pub, said, "No more than thirty minutes, but keep something back. If they really like you, they will want an encore, and you are certain to get more bookings."

When I had finished crafting my repartee, I was quietly

confident that it would be good enough to get a bunch of drunken students laughing or at least to keep them awake.

The following Thursday, I went early to find the venue so as to have a pint and calm my nerves. But no club could I find. I asked a passer-by whether he knew of the club.

"You've got the wrong address, mate. There are two streets with the same name. The place you want is a about half a mile away," he said, pointing me in the right direction.

I trudged from the academic area to the darker side of Liverpool and found the venue, "The Naughty Nipples Club". *Should I run?* No, this was a place that looked like they would find you and make sure you never had children. I went down a flight of stairs into near darkness but, as my eyes adjusted, I discovered the club was packed with middle-aged men, some of whom had kept their raincoats on although, as far as I knew, rain was not forecast.

On my way down the stairs, I passed a door that had The Library painted on it. The barman pointed me to the manger's office. His door was covered in a hand-painted mural of an enormous pair of breasts with large, protruding nipples. Across the impressive embonpoint, somebody had written, "Kenny Lane, the King of Liverpool Light Entertainment."

At some point, no doubt as a tribute to the Beatles, the K had been crossed out and a P inserted.

I knocked.

"Come in."

My first impression was that Kenny was not too fastidious about cleanliness or tidiness and had other virtues that followed godliness. The room was small, badly-lit, with Kenny sitting behind an old, damaged desk with one leg shorter than the other and levelled by copies of magazines. The top one, I noted, was *Snow White Takes the Seven Dwarfs*. Kenny was short, aged about fifty, grossly overweight with a face so pale that it was obvious it had not been in contact with sunlight for many years. Although light on top, he had a broad ponytail. Lying beside him was a sleeping pit-bull terrier.

"Nice dog," I said. "What's its name?"

"Cilla," he replied.

"Does she sing?" I said, trying to impress him with my quick wit.

"Does she bite?"

"Only when I tell her to," he replied with a hint of menace, at which point Cilla opened one eye as if to confirm the truth of that statement.

"Are you married?" I asked nervously, trying to engage him in polite conversation.

"No way, mate. *Shag 'em and leave 'em* is my motto," he replied, confirming that he was not quite ready to settle down in a loving, committed, monogamous relationship. His clothes also reflected the fact that he didn't live with his mum. Kenny's office was made even smaller by the walls being stacked with pornographic magazines which, on closer examination, were produced for different countries.

"Me biggest seller," he said proudly, "an international market."

I thought, to cement our relationship, I should show an interest, so looked with affected curiosity at the shelves. The magazines were arranged alphabetically by country.

"You have a global readership?" I said.

"It's a global product, mate," he said with the passion of a true entrepreneur, "constantly expanding. I am adding a new country every month."

I looked back and indeed it was. The As began with Afghanistan and the stock finished with Venezuela and the Vatican City.

"I refer to it as an art collection," he boasted, "combining the beauty of the body with that of literature."

The largest section was the German one so, again, to ingratiate myself with him, I picked out the top publication. On the front cover was a naked colossus (Koles Riese) named Gunther Grober Schwan – for between his legs hung a phallus of breath-taking length and width, which he affectionately and patriotically called the "Obergruppenfuhrer". The magazine appeared to be designed to showcase Gunther's comprehensive range of interests. It showed him playing golf without a putter, and tennis without a racquet, interestingly double-handed on both sides. The centre pages revealed his avian interest, for it showed Gunther standing in a state of full tumescence with a huge, multi-coloured parrot perched on it, seemingly enjoying an afternoon siesta.

"Impressive," I said to Kenny. "The parrot looks very happy. Did it have a name?"

"Engelbert," he replied. "Gunther loved Engelbert Humperdinck's opera *Hansel and Gretel*. He was also handy on the cello."

Don't ask, I thought.

"They look very happy together," I said, playing to Kenny's obvious love of animals.

"They did," he replied mournfully, "but sadly it came to a tragic end."

"Oh my God," I replied, again trying to be witty, "Did Engelbert bite the pecker that fed him?"

"No," said Kenny ruefully. "Gunther tried to get Engelbert to participate in a threesome with one of Germany's leading adult actresses, Kiera Klitoris."

Engelbert took to it like a duck to water. He told me that when Kiera tried to mount the Obergruppenfuhrer from different directions, one of Kiera's breasts fell on Engelbert, causing fatal injuries. He lived on for a few days. Gunther never left his side, while Kiera sued for damages as her contract didn't include a "feathered creatures" clause.

"But there is no writing in this high-quality example of your art collection?" I said, both out of interest and to further ingratiate myself with a man who was going to give me £20 for 30 minutes' work.

"Gunther was a man of few words," he replied with a sense of intellectual disappointment.

The tribute to Gunther was completed with a large group of athletic young women admiring and enjoying the Obergruppenfuhrer in ways that seemed somehow uniquely German and were not on my mother's list of dangers to look out for. I suspect that Gunther's antics would now be either the stuff of a book or a six-part Channel 4 series encouraging us all to make our sex lives more imaginative.

Looking back I am left with that eternal question: "Does size matter?"

The remaining space on Kenny's walls was covered

by a female tennis player bending over to pick up a ball, although she had obviously, in the course of a particularly exhausting rally, lost both her racquet and knickers.

As we had by now bonded through a common interest in German literature, I felt emboldened to enquire about the library. Did Kenny support and encourage young Liverpool poets? After drinking from a bottle of whisky, Kenny was in a reflective mood.

"Would you like a drop, pal?" he said.

"No, thank you," I replied. "A beer will do."

"Well done, lad," he agreed. "Many a comedian has been ruined by the booze. They finish up forgetting the fuckin' jokes."

"The library has been one of my best ideas," he said with his usual self-confident air.

He told me that it had used to be the Spanking Salon, run by a lovely girl, Sal, married to a plumber with three children. She was an artiste, providing a satisfactory level of arousal with minimal injury. Her most popular routine involved the use of a horsewhip with peacock feathers attached. "Sting and Stroke," she called it, and it was apparently very popular.

"Anyway, after having her third baby, she put on a bit of weight and, unknowingly, was applying rather more force than before. We started getting complaints from the local A&E, and women getting upset when their man was coming home with his arse in shreds.

"Eventually, I had a visit from the boys in blue, threatening to take my licence away. Fortunately, one of our members was a chief inspector locally, and together with £200 and a crate of whisky, they turned a blind eye. But Sal had to leave. I gather she has lost some weight now and is doing home visits. Wonderful mother!

"How to replace a considerable loss of revenue was my problem. So, my brainwave! Most members read the *Sun* with the tasty bird on Page 3 showing her tits. *Let's do it live*, I thought. *A tasty bird reads to the lads.* The art college next door does nude modelling for the students. So, I made enquiries and found a couple of girls studying English at the university who were looking for some extra cash. Well, I tell you, it has been a real winner. You won't believe this, but some of the members have moved on from the *Sun* to more serious reading matter. I warned the girls to steer clear of any erotic material to avoid any unpleasantness and warned the lads that it was a *no touching* activity," Kenny told me nostalgically.

"The effect on some of the regulars has been amazing. Some of the insomniacs have been sleeping like babies after being read "to sleep" by a big girl called April. 'Twitcher', who has suffered from his nerves for years, is as calm as a cat since soft-spoken Katie has been reading about 'Daffodils'.

"What has really blown me away is how popular some of the great popular writers have become, like Charlie Dickins," he said, looking very proud of himself.

"Genius," I said.

"I love chatting to future stars like you," he said. "I hope you remember me when you are looking for a manger. Now, to business, kid. Tonight's sexual and comedic extravaganza. I gather you know the ropes. Stevie, our regular comic, very popular, tells me you have been around. Thursday is always a popular night because it's "Surprise Night", so I am expecting a full house of about 250," Kenny said, and my stomach suddenly fell. "Here's the order of play, lad," he continued, handing me the programme written on what looked like cheap toilet paper. "We kick off with a regular group of artistes who never disappoint, "Linda Leather and the Truncheons". The lads will have a few drinks. Then you go on and give them 30 minutes of laughter before the surprise attraction."

"What's the surprise attraction?" I asked.

"It's an Australian transsexual transvestite production of *The Sound of Music*, performed by a group new to the UK, Shane the Trouser Snake and the Fellatios," he said with a look of excitement.

"But they won't understand what that means," I said.

"That's the point, kid. It's a surprise. If I wrote, "Big Cock Shane and the Blow Jobs", where's the surprise?"

I knew now why Lenny had proved so successful. Masterful! Suddenly, I began to doubt whether my *Wasteland* adaptation would be to the boys' liking. So I decided to invent a serious, longstanding medical condition that required immediate attention to avoid potentially fatal consequences. As I was thinking of which condition to choose – epilepsy, diabetes, heart problem – Kenny took £20 out of his pocket and offered it to me. Dazzled by the sight of so much money, I convinced myself that, although the audience may not be made up of future Nobel Prize winners, they might still appreciate the idiosyncratic nature of the piece.

I have to say that Linda Leather and the Truncheons did not disappoint, and their beautifully choreographed naked satire of Liverpool policing captivated the audience. Kenny gave me a rather over-generous introduction, naming a number of well-known venues where I had appeared and concluding with the words, "So, put your hands together and welcome the next Jimmy Tarbuck."

I was visibly trembling by the time I reached the microphone, holding on to which stopped me from fainting. My act definitely took the boys by surprise, evidenced by the complete silence followed by, "What the fuck is this?"

I saw the heavy glass ashtray too late. I turned, but it caught me behind the ear, rendering me unconscious.

I regained consciousness backstage to the sound of rioting and Kenny pleading for peace with the words, "If you lot don't quieten down, I shall bring the fuckin' comedian back on."

He then offered the audience a free drink.

When Kenny came backstage, he was no longer the same genial scouser.

"What the fuck was all that?" he screamed, looking at Cilla and obviously considering whether more physical damage should be administered.

Feeling the flow of blood, I asked him whether he could get me an ambulance.

"After that pile of shit, you can fuckin' well walk to hospital," he replied unsympathetically, looking like a man who had just come out of a war zone and whose reputation as the King of Liverpool Light Entertainment was seriously under threat.

I grasped a couple more programmes promising "An evening you'll never forget" and made my own way to the hospital, and, after a diagnosis of mild concussion, ten stitches, a bandage and some pain killers, I left to catch my bus home.

Bugger, I thought. I'd left the script behind, and due to subsequent amnesia, my magnum opus was lost forever. *Anyway*, I thought, *I'm £20 better off*. However, as I searched for it, I realised that Kenny, the light-fingered King of Light Entertainment, had reclaimed it while I was flat-out on the floor. No fool, our Kenny.

I never saw the comedian again, but by one of those strange coincidences, I bumped into one of Kenny's barmen who told me that Shane the Trouser Snake and the Fellatios had received a standing ovation and Kenny had signed them up for a European tour in conjunction with his "Book Fairs".

I wonder where they are now. No doubt older, retired, happily married with three children, living off the proceeds of Kenny's entrepreneurial eye, the money shrewdly invested by Shane who went on to qualify as an accountant and had a child who trained as a sex therapist.

The simple, stark reality was that stand-up was a dangerous business for which I was ill-equipped.

"There is a thin line that separates laughter and pain, comedy and tragedy, humour and hurt."

23

The Law It Is

So, I had to ask, *what now?* Finding an answer to this vexing question became more urgent as an increasing number of letters arrived from the bank, which I decided not to open.

Before I had set out on my working life, bankruptcy loomed like a financial vulture. The final throw of the dice had to be my previous nemesis, the law. I decided, as a last resort, to visit the law firms I had not originally written to, and ask to see a partner, fall on my knees, cry, plead, and offer to work for nothing from 6 in the morning, including night shifts.

My first couple of visits resulted in me being escorted to the door by a receptionist who obviously thought they were dealing with a fantasist. Then, at about 4.00pm one Friday afternoon, I walked into the reception of F.M. & Son, a small but successful firm.

"I'm here about articles," I said to the receptionist.

"Of course," she said. "Mr. B. has been waiting for you. Come with me."

What the hell was going on? Was this some sort of divine intervention on my behalf? I thanked God, although, at that stage, he and I had a rather tenuous relationship. I was shown into a huge office decorated and furnished sumptuously in the Georgian style. Sitting at the far end in regal splendour was Mr. B., behind a large Georgian desk. He was heavy, jowly, dressed immaculately as one would expect, with a fine head of hair and a matching moustache. It took some time to reach his desk across an ocean of deep-pile carpet which slowed progress.

"My dear boy," he declared, "do sit down. How are you?"

"Fine, sir," I stammered, trying to conceal an obvious Scouse accent with my finest Ralph Richardson impersonation.

"Sherry, my boy," he asked, pouring two large glasses and drinking half of his before he sat down.

"What a joy to see you. I've heard a lot about you."

God moves in mysterious ways and must have had a word with Mr. B.

"Well," he said, "must catch the train home. Monday start at 9.30. Ten pounds per week."

"Absolutely," I said, left the office and staggered out into the street. What on earth was going on? Had he by some psychic power recognised my potential?

The joy in the modest Bennett household was way

beyond happy and relieved. I had hit the jackpot. Success beckoned. I was to be a professional man, as my mother kept repeating, with a heavy emphasis on *professional*.

I arrived at work on Monday morning early, determined to make an impression, but Mr. B. did not arrive until just after 10.

"Good morning, Jenkins," he said.

"Bennett," I replied.

"Bennett?" he responded, obviously confused.

"Yes, sir. Bennett."

"You are not Christopher Jenkins, the QC's son?" he stammered.

"No, I'm Peter Bennett," I said in the tone of a man doomed for the gallows.

"Good God!" he said. "I have made a terrible mistake. Wait in the reception while I think about it."

I sat for an hour contemplating my fate and the thought of my mother's disappointment, which brought tears to my eyes. The receptionist tenderly offered me a tissue. After an hour, the phone rang.

"Go in," the receptionist said in the voice of someone from the Samaritans.

"This is most embarrassing," my new employer said. "I can't apologise enough. I thought, when you came on Friday, you were Christopher Jenkins, a friend's son. What are we going to do?" He sighed. After another pause that felt like it went on for hours, he went on, "I feel I cannot go back on my word. It would be most dishonourable of me. Who are you?"

"Peter Bennett. I am a graduate, sir."

"My word, you'll bring some intellectual firepower to us, then," he said with no hint of annoyance or disappointment.

I discovered that articled clerks (now trainee solicitors) in those days went for coffee at 11.00 at the local coffee house, so I asked reception where it was and found, to my delight, a group of most congenial young men. No women in those days.

I wandered back to the office full of the joys of spring and optimistic about my future. I had found my place in life.

Mr Bell called.

"Bennett," he said, "in the profession, I call you Bennett. Because you haven't achieved the status of solicitor. However, you must be respected by the staff, so they will call you Mr. Peter."

"Of course, sir," I replied.

"Now, Bennett, a couple of tasks you must undertake every day."

"Anything, sir," I replied, worried that my lack of legal knowledge would be exposed.

"I arrive at the office at 10.00am. You must be here to help me off with my coat and place it, together with my hat [he wore a bowler], scarf and sometimes my umbrella, on the stand in the corner. At 4.00 in the afternoon, I leave the office. You will be here to help me get ready to go home. However, some days after lunch, in the afternoon, I like to have a nap. Please wake me up at 3.45pm, so I don't miss the train."

"Of course, sir."

"Go and get some work from one of the clerks."

In those days most of the work was done by the clerks – now known as legal executives – so I went into the office of the lady who dealt with trusts, Miss S. She was aged about sixty and had a severe, granite-like expression. Her hair was gathered into a tight bun, and she sported a fine moustache. She wore heavily rimmed spectacles and had obviously not smiled for a number of years.

"What's your name?" she asked disdainfully.

"Peter Bennett."

"Well, Mr. Peter," she sneered with a look of utter contempt, "what do you know about trusts and probates?"

"I studied them at university."

"University?!" she exclaimed. "What possible use is that in the practice of law?"

She searched in a pile of papers and, producing a file, she said, "Well, Mr. Peter, here is a file for the estate of one of our smaller clients. Fill in the appropriate forms, let me see them, and then take them to the Probate Division."

Forms have never been one of my strong suits, I'm afraid, so it took me some time, with the help of one of the secretaries (how useful they proved), who called me Mr. Peter.

"Please call me Peter," I said, embarrassed, which obviously pleased her for in every sense she was superior to me.

After lunching at the pub (a place I would visit many times) with my newfound comrades, I presented the documents to Miss S. who glanced at them without comment, and I left for the Probate Office. It was a splendid Victorian building manned by staff steeped in trusts and probates.

I waited in a small queue until it was my turn to present my papers to a man who looked like Bob Cratchit. He briefly perused them and said they were incorrectly completed, with the expression of a man who had seen far too many of these desperately boring documents and took immense delight in finding an error.

"Why?" I stammered.

"It's not for members of staff to advise on legal documentation," he said.

I returned to the office and reported my dissatisfaction to Miss S.

"They say the papers are incorrect," I said.

"So they are," she replied with a glorious sense of satisfaction.

"But what is wrong with them?" I asked.

"You are the graduate, Mr. Peter, not me," she said triumphantly, and I discovered this was her modus operandi. Show her any document, and she would nod without making eye contact and off I would trek to the court to be told it was incorrectly completed by a clerk whose look was that of a judge facing a repeat offender. I could imagine them saying over coffee, "You know that bloke from F. M. and Sons? He is a complete idiot. He'll never pass the finals." You had to work in an office for two years before attempting the final exams.

Again, my hope of redemption was the secretaries who all proved invaluable sources of assistance in my continual battle with the law. I am forever indebted to them.

Mr. B.'s practice consisted of property and trust work for rich and occasionally minor aristocrat clients.

"Don't touch any of the girls," Mr. B. said one day, probably having noticed that I got on well with them. "You are a young man, unmarried. Things can very easily spiral out of control."

He didn't know that I had already found the love of my life, and he seemed to forget his advice at every staff Christmas party.

After a couple of weeks, Chris Jenkins at last arrived, and fortunately, we got on splendidly. However, I did have one small setback on my first Friday. The staff would go to the accounts office where a friendly lady would hand us our wages in a small brown envelope. After my first week, she duly handed it over, and it said £5 less tax.

"I think there has been a mistake," I said. "I was told by Mr. B. that it was to be £10."

"No," she replied kindly. "That was for Jenkins."

I had a job and prospects of a successful and prosperous career. Life was good. At the weekends, I travelled down to Northamptonshire to see my future wife by hitchhiking or standing silently in a train toilet with the door unlocked until the inspector passed by. One day the door opened, but it was another student. On one journey, to my horror, we had a houseful of four.

I shared a large office on the third floor which overlooked the Cavern Club, which we frequented some lunchtimes. It had one major drawback. It was a cellar with no air conditioning. No Health and Safety then, so it was like a sauna, and I returned to the office looking like I had been auditioning for Gene Kelly's *Singin' in the Rain*.

Mr. B.'s Lessons of Life in the Law

Lesson One

Firstly, look as if you are successful. He dressed immaculately, and his office reflected his status as the go-to man in the profession. His extensive knowledge was reflected by his bookshelves lined with copies of the *All-England Law Reports* and textbooks all of which were out of date. This was a man capable of solving even the most difficult legal problems.

He started every consultation with the charm offensive; how were the client's children (whose names he always knew)? This was followed by a glass of sherry and his general reflections about the world at large: the outrageous cost of vegetables or how the city was being ruined by developers ("sharks" he called them). Then another glass of sherry and a thorough update on the client's health, which often lasted long enough to include another glass of sherry. Then to the problem, which the client would explain in some detail. Mr. B. would then offer another glass of sherry, sit back in his chair and gaze at the ceiling for a while, turn back to the client and then talk nonsense with the air of a judge in the Court of Appeal delivering a judgement that was to change of one the fundamentals of English law.

The client would sit, transfixed by Mr. B.'s knowledge, articulateness and sound judgement. Sometimes, Mr. B. would get so carried away with his advice that he would cite non-existent legislation, such as the Bread and Butter Act of 1937. In the silence that followed, you could see the client congratulating himself for choosing the right man for the job, even though he was expensive.

In offering a final glass of sherry and saying goodbye, Mr. B. would provide extra reassurance with the words, "Your worries are over, sleep well and leave everything to us."

The client would leave, floating on a cloud of sherry and relief. Mr. B. would then turn to me without any less self-confidence, say, "So, Bennett, what's all that about?"

"I think it could be something to do with the Trustee Act," I speculated.

"Well, get to work writing an opinion. As long as possible. You can charge more, the longer the advice is. And not too quick or they'll think it was easy."

In those days, the likes of Mr. B. had a relatively short working day. He arrived at the office at 10.10am.

10.00 to 12.30

- Dictation to secretary who meticulously recorded his words of wisdom in shorthand.
- Sign letters or documents prepared by the non-officer corps, including myself. He rarely read them.
- Weigh files. Timesheets had not been invented the, so Mr. B. charged by weight. He would hold the file up and declare 1,000 guineas or, if two lifts were required, 1,500 guineas. I suspect it was as fair as – if not fairer than – today's computerised printouts.

| 12.30. | Leave for lunch or travel to see one of the minor gentry, a task which would always guarantee a decent meal and bottle of wine. |
| 2.30. | On returning from his club, he slept like a baby before catching his train home to Southport at 4.00pm, or a return to the club for some function or other. |

Lesson two

The second thing Mr. B. taught me, after self-confidence, was the power of personal contact. He knew everybody, and everybody knew him. So, about once a week at lunchtime, he would give me a pound and say, "Go and meet people, Bennett. Much more important than knowing law."

During my time with Mr. B., a tragedy occurred which tested my decision-making skills to the full.

Mr. B. had a partner, Mr. L., a bachelor recluse, who was about 55 and belonged to a strict Catholic order. He was apparently clever although, because of his silence, we had no way of knowing for sure. He acted for the Catholic Church in Liverpool, a substantial client. Every day in the morning and the afternoon, he would lie on the floor in his office in the shape of a cross, presumably as a form of penance. He left the door of his office open and would be happy for us to step over him and remove a file on which we were working. He worked long hours and appeared to have no hobbies.

One day, at about 2.45pm, Mr. L, who had earlier done his usual supplication, had a heart attack and died in his office, notwithstanding the efforts of a team of paramedics.

Finally, they gave up and took the body away to get him ready for his celestial journey to the Great Conveyancing Office in the sky.

Mr. B. had a particularly hearty lunch and was sleeping peacefully in his room. I had a decision to make. Do I wake him and tell him the news now or rouse him at his usual time, 3.45pm? *This could be a career-breaker*, I thought. After a few minutes weighing the pros and cons and the staff recovering from the shock (although, I have to say Mr. L. was not liked in the office), I decided. *What would be gained from waking Mr. B. now and denying him a well-earned rest?* Mr. L. was dead and there was nothing we could do. So, I waited until 3.45pm, went to his office and, as I was helping him on with his coat, said solemnly, "Mr. L. has died."

He and Mr. L. had never got on, and never spoke other than on matters of business.

"Well, well," said Mr. B., "must get off. We have people over for dinner."

The following morning, he arrived at his usual time.

"Mr. L. has died, has he?"

"Yes, sir."

"Well, go into his office and see if you can keep things ticking along until I find a replacement."

I entered Mr. L.'s office, which I had rarely visited. It was like a shrine.

So far as we knew, he took his summer holidays in the monastery of a silent order, in the south of France, which overlooked the sea. He obviously wanted to evoke the memory of spiritual upliftment and peace in his office as the ceiling was painted bright blue, the walls yellow, and floor carpet green, I assume reminding him of the sun, sand and the verdant undergrowth.

Mr. B. never mentioned Mr. L. again.

I decided to leave Mr. B. and move to Northamptonshire, nearer my beloved. The train journeys and hitchhiking were proving too stressful and time-consuming, denying the precious time with my heart's desire, as I missed her so much.

"I would be loath to speak ill of any man who I do not know deserves it, but I am afraid he is an attorney."
Samuel Johnson

24

Why Does the NHS Exist?
And Can It Be Changed?

In my final observations about my hospital stay, I think
I should follow Nietzsche's advice and ask the *why*
question. Why do this? Why spend that?

So, why does the NHS exist? And why is it run the
way it is?

1. **It does not exist** for the politicians to argue about,
looking for political advantage and votes. The Secretary
of State for Health is appointed with no experience or
knowledge of the workings or the problems for which he
is responsible. He does the job for a couple of years and
moves on to be replaced by somebody as inexperienced
and/or incompetent. They do more harm than good. One
introduces a policy change costing billions of pounds, the

implementation of which is opposed by the only people who have the knowledge, the medical profession. Doctors and nurses.

Look at former Health Secretary Jeremy Hunt's disingenuous attempt to alter junior doctors' contracts to their disadvantage, using very questionable propaganda. Do politicians really believe that doctors have a set working week, and then spend the weekend relaxing at some grand country house paid for by the taxpayer? As one surgeon said to me, "Say, for example, that my shift is from 8am to 6pm, and an emergency case is admitted. Do I say, 'I'm sorry, I have finished and am off home,'? No, I stay and treat the patient, as long as it takes."

It is often the case that, having already wasted billions of pounds, a new Secretary of State arrives and spends another billion or two on another change that is changed again by the next person in post or because of a new policy.

It sometimes seems that the rule is that if you come to office and announce another £5billion of spending on the NHS, then your job is done. It is like rearranging the deck chairs on the *Titanic*. An article in the Times in November 2020, headlined "NHS management gurus waste millions" provides alarming evidence of both political and managerial waste and incompetence. How many doctors and nurses could have been trained with the vast sums scandalously thrown away?

2. **It does not exist** to allow a large number of overpaid, unenlightened medical managers – whose role is a mystery

to most people – to earn a decent living and be entitled to the usual perks of a car, removal expenses, private medical insurance and a handsome payoff and pension enhancement if they fail.

3. **It does not exist** for subcontractors to make handsome profits, providing a very poor standard of service or going into liquidation, costing the NHS goodness knows how much money. I recently read that 1,300 tons of clinical waste, including body parts and drugs, were left in skips after an NHS contractor (Environmental Waste) went into liquidation. Who negotiated the contract? And has anyone been held responsible for its failure? I have never heard that this was done.

1. **It does exist for... US**. We pay for it, and we are the patients. We are entitled to receive the best medical expertise available, to be treated with respect, compassion, understanding, dignity and love in an environment which is conducive to the fastest possible recovery so we can return to our home and families.

2. **It does exist for... the doctors and nurses and staff** who provide outstanding skill and commitment. The problem is, they are understaffed, underpaid and overworked.

It is only after spending a few weeks in hospital (which, hopefully, most people won't do) that you begin to question the widely held belief that the NHS is "national treasure". As Matthew Parris wrote in *The Times*, "It is not the world's gold standard, as studies have shown, it falls well short of that provided by other countries. We are deceived into believing something that is simply not true by politicians, who are afraid that admitting it requires fundamental major changes will be politically disadvantageous. They are happy to wait for it to collapse (which I suspect it will) rather than risk an electoral backlash for admitting what is self-evident." From my view in the bed, it is obvious that we need, as a priority, thousands more doctors and nurses, staff who are suitably trained and work in an environment which is healthy, uses their outstanding expertise, is rewarding, and which they control and supervise. I was told by many nurses how traditionally the ward sister would manage the ward, including, for example, cleaning and teams that would often stay together for years. No expensive contractors. Is it acceptable that 20 per cent of doctors leave the profession within two years of qualifying? For example, a newly qualified doctor will earn about £25,000 a year, working, I suspect, at least twice the hours of an average employee in the UK. A trainee solicitor in a top London firm (after a three-year degree course and a 12 months final course) will earn £47,000 per annum. The newly qualified consultant, after at least 12 years' further specialist training, will earn less than someone in middle management in the hospital.

A letter in *Private Eye* from a Dr Bernard Maybury provides inside evidence of the problem:

Doctoring numbers

Sir,

Robert Payne (Letters, Eye 1529) attributes the shortage of UK-trained doctors to medical school closures. There have not been any such closures, and in fact 12 new medical schools have opened in the past 30 years, although growth in the medical school places did not historically keep pace with the growing and ageing population.

The more pressing reason for the shortage of home-grown staff is doctors leaving the NHS. I blame the cocktail of heavy workloads, lack of autonomy and uncompetitive salaries combined with professional responsibilities which, if breached, land the clinician concerned in prison. Getting personal, 25 per cent of my medical school cohort (2012) have left the country or left the profession altogether. One of the group, bewilderingly, was awarded an MBE, but it wasn't one of us mugs who stayed.

This is all true of nursing, too, only they've been doubly shafted by the withdrawal of student bursaries.

BERNARD MAYBURY

Something has to change. The new way forward has to be found. As any businessman will tell you, the fact that something worked 20 years ago does not mean that it will work now.

I came across a simple idea recently from a friend who lives in Texas, USA. He has always been a very keen sportsman. Recently, he required a new hip. So, he went to a hospital "run by doctors" who specialize in hip surgery. They operate almost 24 hours a day, and because of their skill and experience, they achieve almost a hundred per cent success rate. You leave the hospital after a day, with excellent follow-up physio. He was running a 5K within 2½ months.

Is the NHS just too big? We have to ask the difficult questions. Should it be broken up into smaller specialist units, such as the one in Texas?

It should definitely be non-political.

We must be brutally honest about the NHS as the employer, the organization. What are its faults and its weaknesses? How can they be improved? As I have described, it takes outstanding long-term leadership.

When I started this journal, I was committed to recording conversations, actions and attitudes in real time as accurately as I could, whether it resulted in praise or criticism. So, as you will have read, it led to perhaps more censure than I had anticipated. Those more experienced than me will have a view but my conclusion from my end of the bed is that working conditions have to change, <u>supervised</u> by doctors and nurses and not management.

As I've indicated, more guidance should be provided (particularly to junior nurses) on how to cope physically, mentally and emotionally with their workload. Are the shifts too long? Are they given proper breaks and advice about diet to maintain the energy levels they require? It was interesting and instructive to watch the nurses on a 13-hour shift. They visibly began to flag – physically and mentally – after about eight hours. Listen to them, ask them what they think. Their views are far more important than those of a man whose previous experience was in catering. Remove what appears to be "failure" among nurses who say, "I love this job, but…"

But how do you fund such changes?

1. As I have said, give authority and control back to the medical staff.
2. Dramatically reduce the number of managers. My instinct after being in business for 45 years is that at least 25% of the management could be cut.
3. If possible, the chief executive should be a medical doctor.
4. Reduce the annual report to no more than 60 pages. As there are no investors to impress, produce it on cheap paper. Make sure it contains clear, useful information – e.g. annual recruitment costs – and write it in language that can be understood by somebody who is not a qualified accountant. Give some copies to ex-patients and ask them whether it makes sense.
5. Take down two thirds of the posters decorating the hospital which nobody reads. I think we all know that assaulting a member of staff is a criminal offence. For essential posters, use cheaper paper or get the children in recovery to draw them.

6. Don't make promises you can't keep.

I am sure that those with more knowledge will be able to think of a lot more.

My health journey continues, but after the stay in the NHS hospital detailed in this book, the antibiotics worked and, hopefully, I have a few more years left. I cannot thank those individuals who looked after me enough, and I hope that this book may, in some way, show my appreciation.

> "The measure of intelligence is the
> ability to change."
> Albert Einstein

Epilogue

My admiration for writers knows no bounds. As Winston Churchill wrote, "Writing a book is an adventure; it begins in amusement, then it becomes a mission, then a master, and finally a tyrant."

My relationship with the medical profession continues and my respect and wonder for their talent and dedication is beyond description. I hope this book may, in some way, show my appreciation.

I am enjoying a comfortable bed, a dark and quiet room without a Scouse drug addict shouting, "No fuckin' Weetabix, the fuckin' telly doesn't work, this place is fuckin' crap!"

I am delighted to report the wife is more subdued.

Sleep tight. Good fortune and particularly good health. And I thank any reader who has got this far.

Addendum

The book is finished. After 10 drafts, many readings and agents' rejections, I am off the sedatives and no longer require psychiatric help. I should be elated or at least relieved. But strangely I am not. The writing of the book appears to have cast a spell on me for a number of reasons.

1. A sense of frustration at how much better the book could have been. As one author wrote, "Writing provokes self-loathing and an immediate desire to rewrite," but

2. It is now too late and I am consumed by my fear of humiliation by the court of public opinion, with either no sales or scathing reviews. In this age of social media will I need to change my name and retreat to a secret location?

3. I have come to realise what a profound effect my stay in hospital has had on me. Nothwithstanding my extensive medical experience, nothing could

have prepared me for all that time on the ward. The long, stressful and lonely days, the lack of sleep, the anxiety about one's fate, the tragedy of other patients' lives, the bed, the noise, the light which turned the environment into a half-seen, half-hidden, dreamlike video recording of my life in which I was cross-examined about beliefs I had held, actions I had taken and decisions I had made.

My mental inquisitor seemed intent on highlighting my failures, my mistakes, misunderstandings and misjudgements, as if any confession I made would wipe the slate clean. It was like Ebenezer Scrooge being visited by Mr. Marley. And a lot of the evidence that my prosecutor produced showed me in an unflattering light, particularly in the early part of my life.

Does suffering have meaning? As my philosophical and psychological guide Victor Frankl says, "To find meaning is the primary motivation of life," and he argues, I believe correctly, that suffering, for example illness, can prove meaningful. Was C. S. Lewis correct when he wrote, "God whispers to us in our pleasures, speaks in our conscience, but shouts in our pains. It is his megaphone to rouse a deaf world"? I hope I may be a better person than I was.

4. Illness, recording my hospital experiences, lifetime memories, the loss of true friends, and age have caused me to face my own mortality. So I decided to write to my grandchildren. As E. M. Forster wrote, "Old age, that seductive combination of wisdom (increased) and

decaying power, where we have fewer potentialities, but something more important, stored realities in the past and these assets cannot be removed." I wanted to share with George, Tabitha and Emelia my "stored realities" without presuming they rise to the level of wisdom. Particularly to highlight my errors so that they may not repeat them. My desire has been fuelled by the world I see around me daily. A world of conflict, violence, hatred, depression and anxiety. An apparent overwhelming existential dissatisfaction with life. The egregious, uncontrolled power of social media companies and "influencers" to disseminate to young people ideas that are toxic and potentially catastrophically dangerous to both themselves and the wider society in which they live.

Young people are confused about what is required to live a meaningful, happy and successful life. In *Alice's Adventures in Wonderland*, Alice asks the Cheshire Cat:

> "Would you please tell me which way I ought to go from here?"
> The Cheshire Cat: "That depends a good deal on where you want to get to."
> Alice: "I don't much care where."
> Cheshire Cat: "Then it doesn't matter which way you go."

Or as Yogi Berra paraphrased it: "If you don't know where you're going, you might end up some place else."

Rudyard Kipling provides us with, I believe, some helpful guidelines:

> I keep six honest serving men
> (They taught me all I knew);
> Their names are What and Why and When
> And How and Where and Who.

> What is the meaning of life?
> Where am I going?
> Who am I?
> What's the point?
> What should I do with my life?
> Who should become my partner/friend?
> What job or career should I pursue or give myself to?

Today I believe young people are being deceived by immoral bad actors (both personal and corporate) where a motive is quite simply one of the deadly sins: *greed*.

Looking at the NHS, I asked the "Why" question. Why does it exist?

So I want to encourage my grandchildren to ask themselves, "What am I here for?" And to answer the questions posed by Rudyard Kipling.

During my lifetime I have seen the rise of a deeply cynical view of life that attempted to provide simple answers to the questions.

"We are on earth to fart about."

—Kurt Vonnegut

"There is only one really serious philosophical question, that is suicide."

—Albert Camus

In the spring of 1975, Michel Foucault, world-famous philosopher, militant and professor at the prestigious Collège de France, took a large dose of LSD. From then on, he believed in taking any risk imaginable, whether it be drugs, sex or any other temptation. Life had no meaning.

"Should I take chances with my life?" a Californian student asked Foucault one day.

"By all means. Take risks, go out on a limb," Foucault replied.

"But I yearn for solutions."

"There are no solutions," he said.

"Then at least some answers."

"There are no answers," Foucault replied. "Sex is worth dying for."

Foucault died young from complications of HIV/AIDS, so could be considered a martyr for his cause.

"The major sin is the sin of being born."

—Samuel Beckett, which seems out of character for a man who played first class cricket.

Friedrich Nietzsche, who believed that we are all potential supermen capable of creating our own destiny, said, "We cannot say, 'It was.' We must live so we can say, 'I willed it.'"

I believe they are profoundly wrong. Philosophers throughout history have tried to provide the answer, which our nihilistic, relativistic world has forgotten, but I quote two who have offered me guidance.

Nelson Mandela said that, "You may find that the cell is an ideal place to learn to know yourself, so search realistically and regularly the process of your own mind and feeling... in judging our progress as individuals, we tend to concentrate on external factors such as one's social position, influence, popularity, wealth and standard of living and education, but external factors may be even more crucial in assessing one's development as a human being: humility, purity, generosity, absence of vanity, readiness to serve your fellow men, qualities within reach of everyone, those are the foundations of one's spiritual life."

Ralph Waldo Emerson advised us all, "To laugh often and much, to win the respect of intelligent people and the affection of children, to earn the appreciation of honest critics and to endure the betrayal of false friends, to appreciate beauty, to find the best in others, to leave the world a bit better, whether by a healthy child, a garden path or a redeemed social condition, to know that even one life has breathed easier because you lived. This is to have succeeded."

My letter to my grandchildren is long but my conclusions are simple. I believe we need to revive the two crucial foundations for a civilized society.

1. An obsession with FACTS and TRUTH.

Senator Daniel Patrick Moynihan (1927-2003) said that, "Everyone is entitled to his opinion but not to his own facts." We appear to be living in a world where we have forgotten the definition of "fact" and "truth".

The suggestion that there can be "alternative facts" is the statement of a deranged, duplicitous mind, a fool or a charlatan or an American Presidential candidate.

Incidentally, I particularly liked a journalist's description of Trump: "He had aspired to and achieved the greatest luxury: an existence unmolested by the rumbling of the soul."

So, if confronted by an alleged "factual statement" or "truth", check it, check it again and maybe once more. I emphasise this point by quoting Dr Deborah Lipstadt, Professor of Holocaust Studies at Emory University, Atlanta, after her crushing victory in the libel case brought by the infamous, discredited and dishonest Holocaust denier David Irving:

> "Truth is not relative.
> We must ask where the evidence is and demand answers.
> There are indisputable facts and objective truths.
> Test them to destruction.

The earth is not flat.
The climate is changing.
Elvis is not alive.
Truth and facts are under assault, defend them aggressively."

And as Galileo taught us, after recanting for the sake of the Church, when he said, "And yet it still moves."

2.   Remember, all we need is LOVE.

Writers have for centuries tried to define it. The Greeks, who were more philosophical than ourselves, restricted it to feelings, not actions, and expressed their feelings in five different ways:

Eros – sexual passion
Ludus – playful love
Agape – love for everyone
Pragma – longstanding love
Philautia – love for oneself

They began the process of writing about love as something mysteriously precious which, more than any other emotion, yielded feelings that appeared to produce an uncomfortable tenderness, devotion and fervent passion for another. So, although it was impossible to define, one could write about the feelings it produced as so many great writers have done for centuries.

We can know that there is no greater feeling than to be

loved, but it also has an adversary: hatred. As strange and mysterious as love. They are like an ethereal vapour which, like a virus, can cause us to behave in a certain way which is, in every sense, the best in us, or as Aristotle called it "Divine"; but has an enemy which is the worst in us, which Aristotle called "Beastly".

As Dr Martin Luther King Jr wrote, "Darkness cannot drive out darkness; only light can do that. Hate cannot drive out hate; only love can do that."

I write this in 2024 and sadly look out at a world where the "Beastly" appears to dominate in many areas of our lives. We are, at the moment, encouraged to allow our subjective desires – for example, sex – to dominate our objective feelings, leading to momentary pleasure, which we believe to be love, but is a psychological deception.

The rules on sexual morality have changed in my lifetime, from the perdition that my mother predicted if my brother or I stepped out of line, to an age where pornography dominates the internet, and you can ring and order a sexual partner to arrive within the hour. So, it can be difficult for different generations to have similar standards. It is, I believe, important that we, the older generation, do not believe that the young behave improperly merely because their behaviour differs from ours. Also, the young must be cautious not to call their elders prudes or puritans because they criticize any new standard of conduct.

I am fascinated by the fact that a large proportion of the psychology profession now appear to be "sexologists" or "sexual hypnotherapists", and bookshelves are full of "self-help" manuals such as *78 Ways of Having an Orgasm in a Volkswagen Golf* or *The Best Sex Parties in Barnsley*. Every newspaper has an "expert" on sex providing weekly advice, for example, "My husband and I have been married for 27 years and have not had sex yet. Is this okay?" Or, "My wife can only have sex in the local library. Is this normal?"

"My boyfriend will only have sex if next door's cocker spaniel is in the room. Is that okay?"

But have these cultural changes and "experts" made our lives happier and more meaningful? Some evidence may suggest not.

The evil of pornography has caused addiction, loneliness and has utterly distorted a healthy view of relationships, evidenced by the appalling rise in violent crime against women.

The increase in sexually transmitted diseases, causing distress to the sufferers and adding to the burden placed on the NHS.

The increase in the number of abortions performed. How many women regret or later suffer psychological problems from making the decision to abort their baby?

The huge amount of money being made by those who, like drug-dealers, feed the addiction to pornography.

The exploitation of women worldwide who are forced into the sex trade.

The social and psychological problems caused by young people watching pornography and being confused about how a healthy relationship should be conducted.

I believe we have been bombarded with propaganda encouraging lust, not love, in films, books and online entertainment channels. We must, I believe, regain a sense of restraint (what Aristotle termed "moderation"), and accept that every desire, however strong, does not produce a healthy and, most importantly, loving relationship.

And finally, I pray in aid of what I have found to be the most inspirational definition of love, written by Viktor Frankl, a copy of which I keep on my desk:

"Love is the only way to grasp another human being in the innermost core of his/her personality. No one can become fully aware of the very essence of another human being unless he/she loves them. By this he/she is enabled to see the essential traits and features of the beloved person; and, even more, he/she sees that which is the potential in the beloved which is not yet actualized. Furthermore, by his/her love, the loving person enables the beloved person to actualize these potentialities. By making him/her aware of what he/she can be and what he/she should become, he/she makes the potentialities come true.

Love is as primary a phenomenon as sex. Normally, sex is a mode of expression for love. Sex is justified, even sanctified as soon as, but only as long as, it's a vehicle of love. Thus, love is not understood as a mere side effect of sex; rather, sex is a way of expressing the experience of that ultimate togetherness which is called love."

I conclude my letter to my grandchildren as follows:

So, what's it all about? Life is living, learning, loving and leaving a legacy. May you find true, long-lasting LOVE in life.

And never forget, LOVE and TRUTH "outweigh the whole world."

Acknowledgements

The medical and hospital staff for providing me with much of the material for this book. The two medical consultants who kindly read the book and reviewed it. For friends who read the manuscript at various stages and offered helpful comments/criticisms, but also gratefully encouragement. And to Karl French, my talented and supportive editor, who miraculously turned a mess of pottage into a book. The blame for the poor quality of the content rests entirely with me.